EARLY AMERICAN DOLLHOUSE MINIATURES

Early American Dollhouse Miniatures

GERALD JENSEN

Photographs by Bill Houston, Jerry Jensen and Jack Jensen

Chilton Book Company   Radnor, Pennsylvania

Words cannot sufficiently express my gratitude to the many friends and relatives who helped with the arduous task of compiling this book. Because of their interest and encouragement, this book became a reality.

Special thanks are due to Bill Houston, for his contribution of time and self, and to my daughter Judy and my sons, Jerry and Jack, for their technical support.

Published in Radnor, Pennsylvania, by Chilton Book Company
and simultaneously in Don Mills, Ontario, Canada,
by Nelson Canada Limited
Library of Congress Catalog Card No. 80-68275
ISBN 0-8019-7023-7 *hardcover*
ISBN 0-8019-7024-5 *paperback*
Designed by Jean Callan King/Visuality
Manufactured in the United States of America
1 2 3 4 5 6 7 8 9 0   0 9 8 7 6 5 4 3 2 1

Contents

Introduction

Building and collecting miniatures is not a recent innovation. In fact, historical records show that miniaturists existed in Europe nearly 450 years ago. In the infancy of this fascinating hobby, European royalty were the predominant force in generating interest and enthusiasm. Craftsmen were commissioned to produce furniture and military miniatures for the collections of royal households. Today's military miniatures, used in table-top war games, are direct descendants of those early European miniatures.

Replicas in miniature have been admired for centuries. Perhaps the most outstanding display is the famous dollhouse built for Queen Mary of England in the early 1920s. Hundreds of craftspeople spent four years creating this world treasure. No detail was spared, from the working water faucet to the real bottled wine in the wine cellar. Even the books in the library contain original, handwritten manuscripts by British authors.

Many well-known miniature houses have been built since the turn of the century. Currently in the United States there are about forty permanent displays of miniature furniture and complete houses in various museums, such as the Colleen Moore dollhouse at the Museum of Sciences and Industry in Chicago, the sixteen-room Thorne display in the Phoenix Art Museum, the Mott Miniatures at Knott's Berry Farm in California (with a display of over 150,000 pieces), and the Washington Dolls' House and Toy Museum in Washington, D.C., which recently celebrated its fifth anniversary.

The small replicas created by early American craftsmen have become desired antiques in the world of today's miniatures. These heirlooms were produced at a time when miniatures were stereotyped as dollhouse furniture and considered strictly for little girls. How times have changed! A recent newspaper ad offered a dollhouse in Texas for $30,000, one indication that dollhouses and miniature furniture have made the transition into the adult world and can no longer be considered toys for children.

In the early 1970s, interest in miniatures rose greatly as a result of the awareness generated by the Bicentennial displays. Nostalgic memories of yesteryear were awakened when federal, state and local agencies sponsored tributes to the pioneers of America. Statewide programs were held throughout the year, and many cities and towns celebrated with parades, folk dances, and concerts. Buttons, pins, and paraphernalia of every description, depicting all the national historic sites, were sold. Miniature statues of the Minutemen, the Liberty Bell, and the Statue of Liberty appeared everywhere.

Today, the ever-expanding interest in miniatures includes an untold number of people, novice to artisan, from all walks of life and all age groups, who enjoy the big world of tiny things. Miniature furniture building and collecting is now the fastest-growing hobby in the United States.

When I became interested in miniatures and wanted to build them, finding plans for certain pieces of Early American furniture was difficult because few if any plans were available at the time. It soon became apparent that if I were going to build miniatures, I would need to create my own sets of plans first.

This book is a response to that challenge, providing plans for the enthusiast—from beginner to advanced craftsman—to enjoy the hobby of miniatures by creating his or her own collectible treasures.

There are many different ways to enjoy the world of miniatures. Some people derive pleasure studying the craftsmanship of miniature displays. They spend many hours window shopping at various shops and crafts fairs. Others enjoy collecting the works of miniature builders, continually searching out high-quality, handcrafted miniatures. A good collection may be assembled this way very quickly, but acquiring each piece can become expensive.

Still others choose to build their miniatures themselves. Although this approach may be the most satisfying, it also requires much time and a considerable investment in workshop tools. An alternate approach, and probably the most realistic, is to build as many miniatures as possible and purchase the rest. This provides the most enjoyment in building miniatures and the least expense in collecting them. The approach you choose will be decided on the basis of your personal preference, available time, and budget.

After being involved with miniatures for a while, you probably will want to become more involved in this fascinating hobby. The excitement of establishing a collection can turn even the casual builder into an enthusiastic miniaturist. This book was intended to help you enjoy the world of miniatures by making plans available for you to build and collect your own handmade miniatures.

CHAPTER 1

Woods, Stains, and Finishes

WOOD

Many woods are suitable for miniature furniture building. The choice in the variety of wood is determined by availability and personal preference. Some miniaturists use hardwoods—walnut, oak, or mahogany—for building miniatures. The beauty of these woods is accentuated when a hand-rubbed finish is applied. Other miniature artisans work primarily with balsa because of the ease with which this wood can be cut and shaped. (See Fig. 1–1 for an assortment of hardwoods and softwoods.)

Better hobby and craft stores and miniature specialty shops stock an adequate supply of assorted woods in sheets and strips, along with a large assortment of moldings. If you have difficulty ob-

3

Fig. 1–1 Wood Assortment

taining lumber locally, you may wish to contact one of these mail-order suppliers.

Craftsman Wood Service
2727 So. Mary St.
Chicago, IL 60608
(*catalog available*)

Albert Constantine and Sons
2050 Eastchester Rd.
Bronx, NY 10461
(*catalog available*)

There are several considerations you should keep in mind before selecting wood for any project.

1. Before beginning any project, make certain you have enough wood in *all* the required thicknesses.
2. Select wood with a small, straight grain. Wood with a large, irregular grain looks out of scale. Use large-grained boards as backs or inside supports, where the grain will not be noticeable.
3. All boards have one side smoother than the other. Try to keep the smooth side for the exposed surface. Otherwise, you will need to do considerable sanding to get a smooth surface.

4. The most commonly used wood sizes are $\frac{3}{32}$ and $\frac{1}{8}$ inch thick. Save unused portions from large projects for use on small ones.
5. Thicknesses vary from board to board. Using boards that are as close as possible to the same thickness will help to reduce mismatched parts.
6. Boards have saw-cut edges when you purchase them. Allow for this when cutting the pattern.
7. To prevent wood from splitting when you drive a nail, drill an undersized hole first and then drive the nail.

The following is a brief description of the various types of wood available and their recommended use in building miniatures.

BASSWOOD

For all-around use in miniature projects, I recommend basswood, a light, open-grained wood that is easily worked with saw or knife and easy to sand. It can be stained or painted any color without raising the grain of the wood, which is an important feature to the quality-minded miniaturist. It is inexpensive and available in a full range of thicknesses, from $\frac{1}{32}$ to $\frac{1}{4}$ inch and in 2, 3, and 4 inch widths. It is used by most manufacturers of dollhouses as accessories for windows, doors, railings, structural shapes, and picture-frame moldings. Most hobby and craft stores stock ample supplies all year round.

CHERRY

This is a fine, reddish brown, cabinet-grade wood. It can be cut easily with a jigsaw, table saw, or knife. A nice finishing wood with a rich sheen, cherry is ideal for projects like the trestle table and benches. Cherry is not as available in the full range of sizes as basswood is. It is also slightly more expensive, but when you consider the amount of wood used in each project, the additional cost is insignificant.

WALNUT

This wood has a rich, chocolate-brown color, is fairly easy to work with, and develops a fine finish. Walnut is slightly more expensive than basswood and not available at all hobby and craft stores in a full range of sizes, although some specialty shops stock the thicknesses required for building miniatures. The character of this wood adds a distinctive appearance to any project.

BALSA

This is a light, grey-toned wood that is extremely soft and easy to cut and carve with a knife. Balsa does not have much strength and is easily dented. Inexpensive and available at all hobby stores, it is recommended for most carving projects.

POPLAR

This is a cream- to tan-colored wood, similar to basswood but slightly softer. Poplar cuts well with a knife or saw, but stain tends to raise its grain. Moderately priced and available from lumber dealers, it is suitable for most miniature projects.

MAHOGANY

This is a deep reddish brown wood that is fairly easy to cut with a saw and fin-

ishes well. It is not as available as other woods and is slightly more expensive. Mahogany, considered by many the monarch of woods, is a fine selection for exposed cabinet work.

OAK

This is a greyish brown wood that is extremely hard and therefore difficult to work with. Because it has a coarse grain, it is not recommended for use by beginners.

AROMATIC CEDAR

This is a reddish brown wood with streaks of cream. It is easily cut and sanded and should have a natural finish to expose its beauty. Moderately priced, it is not always available in all thicknesses. It is an ideal selection for the blanket chest and lamp projects.

SUGAR PINE

This is a cream-colored, open-grained wood. Sugar pine is reasonably priced and available at lumber yards and do-it-yourself centers in $\frac{1}{2}$ and $\frac{3}{4}$ inch thicknesses. It can be cut and sanded easily. It is used primarily for dollhouse moldings and door and window construction. Because of its softness, sugar pine is recommended for projects requiring carving.

KNOTTY PINE

This is a grey-toned, brown-colored wood. Available at lumber yards in standard $\frac{3}{4}$ inch thickness, knotty pine is best suited for shingles on a dollhouse or as wall paneling to accent small areas.

STAINS

There is an unlimited range of suitable stains on the market today: water-based, vinyl-based, and oil-based stains in liquid form. Several brands of stains are also available in spray cans. These have the advantage of drying usually in less than 30 minutes. They are useful in spraying odd-shaped assemblies with tiny nooks and crannies. I have obtained the best results from a good quality oil-based stain. Several good brands, in a variety of colors, are available at hardware and lumber stores. Fruitwood, antique walnut, colonial maple, and tavern pine are the stains used on the miniature furniture described in this book.

Be sure to mix stain thoroughly before using to prevent uneven color. To stain many small pieces, fashion a small basket from a piece of window screen, submerge the parts in the basket into the can of stain, remove, and wipe dry with a cotton cloth. A second coat may be necessary on small hardwood pieces. For large pieces, apply stain with an inexpensive brush and then dry with a cotton cloth before gluing pieces together. To keep wood from warping on large pieces, remove excess stain with a cotton cloth and place the piece on a flat surface under weights until dry.

PAINTS

Most shops specializing in miniatures stock a wide selection of quality paints and stains. Colors range from soft pastels to bright solids for exterior and interior decorating. Stain and paint are available in a spectrum of colors and available in various quantities, from ounces to pints. Quick-drying paints are available in jars and spray cans.

Acrylic artist paints, used for painting the pictures shown in Chapter 8, are mixed with water to the proper consistency.

FINISHES

To eliminate brush strokes and puddling, apply the finishing coat with a spray can of satin finish polyurethane for a semigloss sheen. Apply the final finishing coat after the miniature is assembled. Best results can be obtained with an old knife and blade. Attach the blade firmly to the underside or back of the miniature; this will enable you to move the piece in all directions while applying the finishing coat. Buff lightly with steel wool, and apply a second coat if desired.

Another finish may be obtained by mixing one part shellac with one part denatured alcohol and applying with a small artist's brush. Buff lightly with fine steel wool. Repeat if desired.

CHAPTER 2

Tools

When they first decide to pursue a hobby building miniatures, some people feel compelled to rush out and purchase every hand and power tool in existence. One word of caution: DON'T. A workshop that is overflowing with all the latest innovations in power equipment and hand tools does not guarantee success in every project. Acquire the tools as you need them, buying the best your budget allows. This applies to hand tools as well as to power tools.

The following list of recommended power tools is intended as a reference only. This list is based on the tools that were used to build the miniatures in this book. To help your selection, brief descriptions are included.

POWER TOOLS

table saw: Any reliable table or radial saw with an 8 inch (or less) diameter blade is satisfactory, provided it is accurate. A plywood-cutting veneer blade is strongly recommended; it is narrow and gives a smooth cut that requires very little sanding, making it ideal for miniature work. Because a table saw is used in nearly every project, purchase one of good quality.

jigsaw: Just about any jigsaw is satisfactory because most of the lumber will be $\frac{1}{4}$ inch or less in thickness. Narrow, thin jigsaw blades are recommended because of the sharp cuts that are required on some projects. A wide selection of good jigsaws is available; the Dremel Moto Shop is an excellent choice. (Fig. 2–1.)

electric drill: Any good quality $\frac{1}{4}$ or $\frac{3}{8}$ inch size drill will do. It is used in conjunction with a drill stand to produce the contoured chair seats. Most drill stands are adjustable and will fit any drill. Use where a large number of drilled holes are required.

wood lathe: Either a standard wood lathe or the Dremel Moto Lathe are acceptable. Although you can do without a lathe, you will find your projects simpler with one. A lathe can also be used to make wooden bowls and trays.

Dremel Moto Tool: This tool is indispensable for drilling a large quantity of holes.

HAND TOOLS

Hand tools are usually selected on the basis of personal preference. The following hand tools are recommended for miniature building.

X-Acto knives: #1 and #5

X-Acto knife blades: #10, 11, 16, and 24

pin vise in two sizes

drill bits: sizes $\frac{1}{32}$, $\frac{3}{64}$, $\frac{1}{16}$, $\frac{3}{32}$, #60, #76, and #72

router bit: size H66

coping saw

small files (jeweler's or needle): $\frac{1}{8}$ round, $\frac{3}{32}$ round, tapered, 3-cornered, and flat

small pliers: needle nose, flat head, and side cutter

Fig. 2–1 Cutting Pattern with a Jigsaw

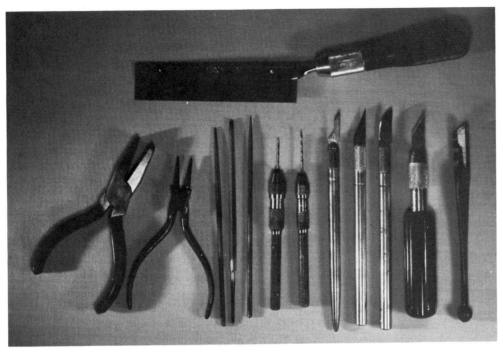

Fig. 2–2 Assortment of Hand Tools

Fig. 2–3 Circle Template, 6″ Ruler, and Pens

hammer

6 inch ruler (graduated machinist's preferred)

12 inch ruler

yardstick

small vise, portable

compass

awl

circle template (plastic draftsman)

tri square or combination square

bench vise

C-clamps: 1, 1½, and 2 inch

tweezers

scissors

glass cutter

miter box

woodburning pen

soldering iron

Knife handles and blades are essential for making spindles, carving decoys, and shaping violins and guitars.

Use the pin vise for drilling holes. If many holes are required, use an electric drill or Dremel Moto Tool.

Miniature files are useful in shaping spindles. Buy an inexpensive set of jeweler's or needle files.

The 6 inch metal machinist's ruler is graduated in 32nds and 64ths, making it useful for miniature work.

A try square is useful for squaring the ends of boards and for laying out patterns.

A circle template is handy for drawing circles or corner radii.

Tweezers are useful for installing drawer pulls, handles, and brads, and for retrieving small dowels.

Use the woodburning pen to decorate the front of the blanket chest, violin, and guitar.

OTHER TOOLS

In addition to the hand and power tools, the following miscellaneous items are helpful.

glue

sandpaper, fine and extra-fine

emery cloth, 200 and 400 grit

pencils

graph paper

carbon paper

craft ribbon pins, ⅝ inch long for nails, 1½ inch long for spinning wheel

copper wire, sizes AWG 18, 24, and 28

crochet thread, size A65

black thread, size 50

fishing line, black cotton

rubber bands

artists' brushes

clothespins, spring type

razor blades, single edge

wood putty

masking tape

nails

carpet tacks

paint brushes

stain, oil base

paint, flat black and white

rivets

toothpicks

cotton swab sticks (wood)

hardware: craft pins, door knobs, drawer pulls, miniature nails, butt hinges, and hinge blanks

There are other items you will need as you expand your accessories. Buy them as you need them.

SALVAGE AND SAVE

Start a salvage drive to acquire items for miniature building. First obtain several shoe boxes and plastic parts boxes to hold the loot (see Figs. 2–5 and 2–6). Once you become involved with miniatures, things in the real world take on a different dimension. Items that were once discarded without a second thought now gain a new lease on life as something useful and valuable in the miniature world.

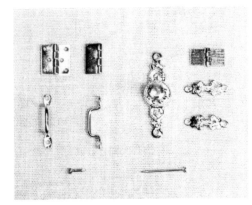

Fig. 2–4 Purchased Hardware Items

The following is a list of suggestions.

rubber bands—They make an excellent substitute for glue clamps. The $\frac{3}{8}$ inch wide can be used for gluing furniture pieces.

Fig. 2–5 Accessory Box

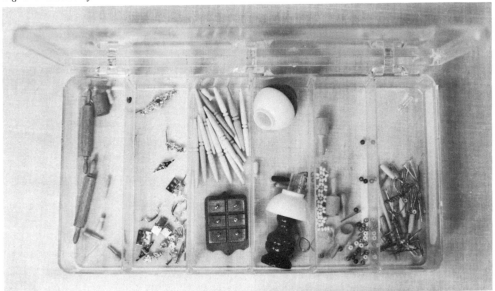

11

clothes pins—The spring-type clothes pin is another fine substitute for a small glue clamp. When used with a rubber band, it makes an ideal picture-frame clamp.

fishing line—black waxed cotton, 8 to 16 lb. test, makes good telephone or extension cords.

fishing bobber—The two-tone red and white type. Available in many sizes, from $\frac{3}{4}$ to $1\frac{1}{2}$ inch diameter, these make excellent lamp shades. Use the $\frac{3}{4}$ inch diameter ones for desk lamps and the larger ones for table lamps.

straight pins—The craft type. Ribbon pins are gold colored and make a fine miniature nail. Cut pin $\frac{3}{8}$ inch long for a fine small nail. Take the remaining piece, file the

cut end flat, and you have a fine finishing nail.

plastic sheets—Clear plastic is available as credit card holders, photo covers, etc. and can be used for picture-frame glass or windows for dollhouses.

plastic tubes—Use for glass chimneys on desk and table lamps. Available in a variety of sizes as holders for replacement erasers and display tubes for drill bits.

Monopoly pieces—Discarded wood-turned pieces make excellent lamp bases.

beads—The small beads used for Indian bead work. The white and black ones make porcelain drawer pulls when used with ribbon pins.

Fig. 2–6 Accessory Box

paint brush—A discarded nylon paint brush is ideal for kitchen and fireplace brooms.

gift wrap—There are many fine wrapping papers with suitable miniature designs. Save for lining trunks, shelves, and drawers, and for wrapping miniature Christmas gifts.

friction tape—Used as a flexible hinge to simulate leather. Cut diamond shaped, $\frac{3}{8}$ inches long and $\frac{3}{16}$ inches wide.

masking tape—Makes good hardware on steamer trunks. Can be cut to any shape to form hardware.

aluminum tape—Use for hardware and as reflectors on sconces, etc.

carpet tacks—Special type with domed head, $\frac{1}{8}$ inch diameter. Paint flat black and use as drawer pulls.

brass shim stock—Available from automotive stores in thin stock, .001 to .005, for making hardware. Use as screen panels on old-fashioned pie cupboard.

used jigsaw blades—A saw blade in miniature.

brass beads—The type found on key chains. Use for drawer and door pulls. Attach with straight pin.

rivets—Hollow brass and copper rivets make individual candle cups for sconces and candle holders.

solid rivets—The $\frac{1}{4}$ inch diameter makes a bell for an antique telephone. Use larger ones for lamp bases.

crochet thread—Suitable for caning material, miniature macrame, and wall hangings.

copper wire—Any size is usable, from $\frac{3}{32}$ inch diameter to the smallest you can find. Use for violin and guitar pegs, lamp and wall brackets, and rug beaters.

music wire—Variety of sizes available. Can be used for guitar strings, potato masher, and whisk.

craft sticks or popsicle sticks—With squared ends make a desirable wainscoting. Stain to desired color and attach with glue, cap with chair rail moulding.

paint cans—Quart size can is useful for shaping back panels for chairs and rockers. Cut desired pieces to required size, soak in warm water ten minutes, and attach to can with rubber bands. Allow to sit overnight and parts will dry to curved shape.

foam rubber—The $\frac{3}{8}$ inch thick size is suitable for mattresses; the $\frac{1}{4}$ inch thick for pillows.

round toothpicks—They make tapered candles. Cut one inch long, sand smooth, paint flat white, and attach a piece of black thread for burned wick. Buff with a bar of parafin for a waxy feel.

cotton-tipped (wooden) swabs—These make good broom handles and are excellent for stringers on the deacon's bench.

CHAPTER 3

Building Miniatures

The most important point to remember about miniature building is that practically all craftsmen once started as novice builders. Time, desire, and effort are the ingredients that transform beginners into accomplished miniaturists. If you take the time, possess the desire, and put forth the effort, you too can become successful.

The first attempt you make at building miniatures may not produce a museum piece, but your second attempt will be better than your first, and your third will be a big improvement over your second. The progress between your first attempt and your third is called experience. Remember: There are no failures in miniature building, only various degrees of success.

The longer you devote to working with miniatures, the more critical you will become when evaluating the works of other craftspeople or assessing your own efforts. The miniaturist soon becomes acutely aware of the various features that constitute a quality miniature and is able to differentiate between mass-produced items and those pieces built with care and patience.

Appearance, proportion, and detail are the features a miniaturist looks for when he or she searches out quality miniatures. Appearance is important, for each piece should be presented as attractively as possible. Color and finish contribute to the aesthetics of the miniature. Proportion, or scale, is another element in determining the quality of a miniature. If the piece is out of proportion, its beauty is lost, and no amount of finishing can reclaim it.

The third element, detail, or method of construction, is not always evident at first glance. Many furniture pieces contain some unusual construction detail, such as mortise and tenon joints, working drawers and doors, contoured seats, caned seats, doweled joints, hinge pins, and curved backs. A mortise and tenon joint or a pegged crossbrace not only improves the appearance of a piece but also adds structural integrity. Working doors and drawers on various pieces add a touch of realism, as do contoured seats. Caned seats are reminders of yesterday's craftsmen and add to the appearance of the miniature. A chair table would not have the appeal it does were it not for the wooden hinge pins and the operating drawer. In fact, much of the intrigue of miniatures is in their realistic detail.

Appearance, proportion, and detail were the major considerations taken in building the furniture from which the plans in this book were developed. To minimize the difficulty in building some of these miniatures and still maintain the individual characteristics of each piece, some liberties have been taken with the details of construction. For that reason, this book should not be construed as a period furniture historical document. The plans presented here were created as accurately as possible. The intent, however, was to provide plans for anyone who wants to enjoy miniature building as an avocation.

Building miniatures from scratch, whether a complete houseful or a few special pieces, is a rewarding hobby, measured by the sense of accomplishment one gains in making something by hand oneself. It is challenging in many respects, but it is also a relaxing and enjoyable pastime. It has been so for me, and it can be for you too.

SCALE AND DIMENSIONS

Scale is defined as the ratio of the reduced miniature dimension to the original full-sized measurement. There are several different scales used in building miniatures.

The most universally used and accepted scale in miniatures is the $\frac{1}{12}$ scale. That is, every inch in miniature-sized furniture is equal to 12 inches (one foot) of the full sized prototype. All the plans in this book are to the $\frac{1}{12}$ scale.

In the United States, the basic unit of measurement for length is the inch. This system is divided into two categories, decimal and fractional. The fractional form $1\frac{1}{2}$ inches is equal to the decimal 1.5 inches.

With few exceptions, all the material utilized in the construction of miniatures is available in fractional form (i.e. $\frac{1}{32}$, $\frac{1}{16}$, $\frac{3}{32}$, $\frac{1}{8}$, $\frac{1}{4}$ inch, etc.). Exceptions are shim stock, wire, and nails or brads, which are available in decimal form equivalent.

Wire is specified by gauge size. The gauge size indicates the wire diameter.

15

The larger the gauge number, the smaller the wire diameter. Thus, a 30 gauge wire is .010 inch diameter, and a 24 gauge wire is .020 inch diameter.

Small nails and brads are specified by diameter and length. Brads appear as "1″ 17 Ga.", which means the brad is one inch long and 17 gauge (.045″) diameter.

To help reduce the confusion between decimal and fractional dimensions, the following chart shows fractional, decimal, and scale equivalents.

FRACTIONAL DIMENSION	DECIMAL DIMENSION	SCALE DIMENSION EQUIVALENT
$\frac{1}{64}$	.016	$\frac{3}{16}$
$\frac{1}{32}$	.031	$\frac{3}{8}$
$\frac{1}{16}$	.062	$\frac{3}{4}$
$\frac{3}{32}$	.093	$1\frac{1}{8}$*
$\frac{1}{8}$	.125	$1\frac{1}{2}$
$\frac{5}{32}$	.156	$1\frac{7}{8}$
$\frac{3}{16}$	.188	$2\frac{1}{4}$
$\frac{1}{4}$	.250	3
$\frac{3}{8}$	.375	$4\frac{1}{2}$
$\frac{1}{2}$	.500	6

*Some miniature builders use this for a 1″ dimension.

ABBREVIATIONS

The following abbreviations are used in the project detail and assembly drawings.

AWG	American Wire Gauge standard size
℄	center line of part
d or dia.	diameter
r or rad.	radius, radii
r.h.	right hand
l.h.	left hand
dp	deep
l	length
pc	piece
sq	square
w	width

ACCURACY

DIMENSIONAL ACCURACY

There are several schools of thought on just how exact the dimensions of miniatures should be. One group believes that if it fits in the doll house, that's close enough. Fortunately, not many miniaturists ascribe to this theory. The extreme purists believe that the miniature must be the exact replica of its full-sized counterpart in every respect. This is an ideal philosophy, and of course it has its limitations.

Being realistic lies somewhere in between. Consideration has been given in this book to making the dimensions as accurate as possible for each project and still allowing it to be reproduced.

PATTERN LAYOUT AND TRANSFER

For square or rectangular parts, draw the pattern directly on the reverse side of the board with a light pencil line, using an accurate ruler and try square. Verify dimensions before cutting the board.

For irregularly shaped parts, such as the base trim and sides of the hutch and desk, trace the pattern as accurately as possible on onion skin or graph paper. Tape the pattern to the selected board, insert carbon paper, and transfer the pattern to the reverse side of the board, as shown in Fig. 3–1. Graph paper with grid lines is recommended; use the grid lines to maintain squareness when drawing and transferring the pattern. Keep

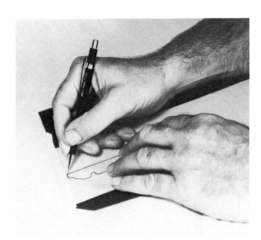

Fig. 3–1 *Transferring Project Pattern*

the use of carbon paper to a minimum, using it only for odd-shaped pieces. This not only will assure better accuracy but, more importantly, will reduce the amount of sanding required to remove the carbon paper lines.

CUTTING IDENTICAL RECTANGULAR SHAPES

Use the rip fence on the table saw to produce identical pieces. Adjust the rip fence to the specified dimension and proceed to cut the required number of pieces. This provides a greater degree of accuracy than does cutting each piece individually.

CUTTING IDENTICAL IRREGULAR SHAPES

After the pattern has been transferred to one board, tape the required number of boards together with masking tape, and then cut the pattern. This will give you identical parts. Remember to reverse

one board so the exterior surface is the smooth surface on both boards.

LOCATING HOLE PATTERNS

Establish the hole pattern as accurately as possible. Then use an awl to make a slight impression on the board or spindle to start the drill bit. Remember not to drill too deep.

SANDING FLAT PIECES

Wrap a piece of fine sandpaper around a small block of wood to sand straight edges and surfaces.

SANDING IRREGULAR SHAPES

Wrap a piece of fine sandpaper around a dowel to shape and sand irregular edges. For identical shapes, tape both pieces together and then sand.

SOME FURTHER SUGGESTIONS

The following points are suggested to help you improve the quality of the miniatures you build and thereby increase your satisfaction in building them.

1. Start with less complicated projects and build confidence while improving craftsmanship before attempting more difficult ones.
2. Check dimensions carefully. Accuracy in measuring is one of the most critical aspects in building well-made miniatures. Quality miniatures would be rare indeed if accuracy were ignored. Reasonable care in establishing dimensions is all that is necessary.
3. Stain parts before gluing. Glue has a tendency to seal the wood, which prevents the stain from penetrating the

17

wood. More than one piece has been ruined because of uneven staining and no amount of sanding will remove the effects of the glue.

4. Whenever possible, dry assemble parts to check for fit before gluing, so that any final corrections can be made easily. After the glue has dried, it is impossible to correct an error without affecting the appearance of the piece.

5. The most essential attribute a miniaturist can develop is *patience*. It takes less time to do it right the first time than to try to adjust for mistakes or redo the piece from scratch.

CHAPTER 4

Techniques

Techniques are different approaches to solving the same problems. There are as many different techniques being devised and applied in the manufacture of miniatures as there are craftsmen who enjoy designing and building them. A particular technique that works well for one person may not work at all for another. Trial and error is probably the best way to learn which methods work well for you.

The methods shown here for making spindles for benches and chairs, fixtures for contoured seats, and caning for chairs demonstrate the craftsmanship that went into building the miniatures in this book.

SPINDLES FROM STANDARD DOWELS

Most small commercial doweling is elliptical, not round, due to the manufacturing process. Because of this, it is difficult to produce spindles with a groove of uniform depth on a wood lathe or even a fine jeweler's lathe. A lathe can be used, however, if you start with an oversized dowel and reduce the diameter over the complete length of the dowel.

An easier approach is to cut a groove with a knife. With a knife, the depth of the cut can be made uniform even on an elliptical, out-of-round dowel. And, since most spindles are tapered anyway, they can be shaped round in the process of tapering the spindle.

Obtain wood dowels from a craft shop or hobby store. Or buy wooden meatskewers from your meat market. They are $\frac{5}{32}$ inch diameter, which makes them exactly $1\frac{7}{8}$ inch diameter in scale and just right for the chair legs in most of the projects in this book. The skewers are either birch or maple, and both can be cut easily with a sharp knife and shaped with a file or sandpaper.

SHAPING SPINDLES

Select a dowel of the desired diameter, square one end, and cut to the required length. Measure the groove centers, mark with a pencil, and then circumscribe a pencil line around dowel. (Use a piece of masking tape wrapped around the dowel as a guide.) Draw a straight line to prevent the spiral effect that can be produced by freehand line work; this line will locate the center of the groove. Next, make a parallel line on both sides of the groove center (Fig. 4–1) to indicate the width of the groove. Make the width of the groove as narrow as possible at first; it can be widened later.

Cut a shallow V-cut all around the dowel with a sharp knife, following the lines in Fig. 4–2. Then locate the next

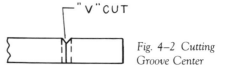

Fig. 4–2 Cutting Groove Center

groove and repeat the marking and cutting. When the second cut is complete, the spindle should look like either A or B in Fig. 4–3, depending on the spacing of the grooves.

The various styles of spindles discussed here are shown in Fig. 4–4.

Style A: This style is formed with the method previously described. It is used on small spindles and where space is limited.

Style B: Start with the basic V-shaped cut, and then round the corners with a knife or file. Shape the taper with a knife, and then sand smooth. This style is suited best for legs and uprights on chairs and benches. (See Fig. 4–5.)

Style C: Starting with the basic V-shaped cut, use the thin edge of a tapered file to shape a flat area and form round corners. Then taper with a knife and sandpaper. This is the most professional-looking spindle but the most difficult.

Style D: Start with the basic V-shaped cut, and then shape with a small, round file. The width of the groove will be determined by the size of the file used. For larger grooves, wrap sandpaper around a dowel and sand proper depth.

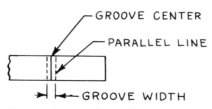

Fig. 4–1 Locating Groove Center

Fig. 4–3 Spindle Cut Detail A and B

20

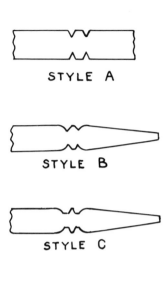

STYLE A

STYLE B

STYLE C

STYLE D

Fig. 4–4 Styles of Spindles

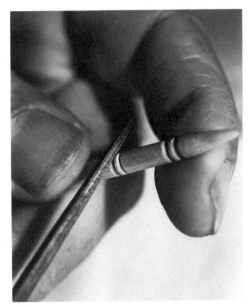

Fig. 4–5 Spindle Shaping with a File

DUPLICATING SPINDLE PATTERNS

To duplicate the spindle patterns on projects that require identical spindles, measure and cut the first spindle as accurately as possible. Then, using the first spindle as a template, transfer the configuration of each groove to the remaining spindles. This will yield a better duplication than measuring each spindle individually.

SPINDLE END SIZING FIXTURE

If the grain of the wood is not straight, attempting to cut, say, a $\frac{3}{64}$ inch diameter on the end of a toothpick can be frustrating. A lot of problems can be eliminated by making the sizing fixture shown in Fig. 4–6. Any scrap piece of hardwood will do. Drill $\frac{3}{64}$, $\frac{1}{16}$, and $\frac{3}{32}$ inch diameter holes into the edge of the

wood. To size a dowel, shape a slight taper on the end of the dowel, and with a twisting motion insert it into the proper hole. This will produce a symmetrical, stepped dowel with the correct diameter on the small end. Slight trimming with a knife at the shoulder will improve the appearance. Or trim to the desired length and use as is.

CHAIR SEAT CONTOUR FIXTURE

All of the chair projects in this book, including the rocking chairs, can be built without contoured seats. Because of the difficulty involved in making a contoured seat, it may be better to build these with flat seats at first. Once you have become adept at building miniatures, however, you will want to attempt

21

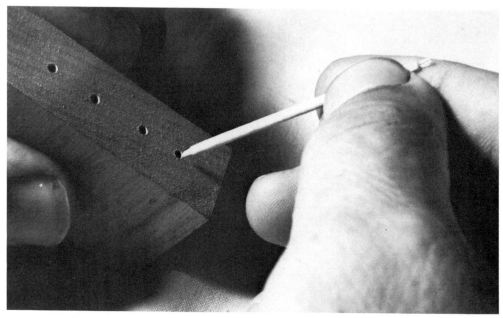

Fig. 4–6 Spindle End Sizing Fixture

the contour seat to add that finishing touch of craftsmanship to your chair projects.

An electric drill and a table top stand are required to make contoured seats, in addition to the fixture shown in Fig. 4–7. (The pattern for the contour fixture is in Fig. 4–8.)

MATERIALS

PART		DIMENSIONS	QUANTITY
A	*Top*	$\frac{1}{2} \times 3 \times 4$	1
B	*Base*	$\frac{1}{2} \times 4 \times 6$	1
C	*Guides*	$\frac{3}{32} \times \frac{3}{8} \times 1\frac{1}{2}$	2
D	*Bolts and Nuts*	#10 – 1½ long	2 ea.

CONSTRUCTION

1. Cut top item **A** to pattern (Fig. 4–9). Locate holes in approximate location shown.

2. Cut base item **B** to pattern (Fig. 4–8). Then use top **A** as a drill guide and drill matching $\frac{3}{16}$ inch diameter holes. Then counterbore on the bottom side for the bolt heads to fit flush.

3. Cut guides **C** to pattern (Fig. 4–8).

Fig. 4–7 Contour Fixture

Fig. 4–8 Pattern for Contour Fixture

ASSEMBLY

4. Position guides **C** at dimensions indicated by dotted lines on underside of top **A** (Fig. 4–9), and attach temporarily until final position is established for a symmetrical pattern on chair seat blank. Assemble (Fig. 4–10).

5. Install bolts **D** flush with bottom of base **B**.

6. Place top **A** over bolts, and add nuts loosely.

The contour jig accommodates a

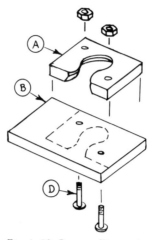

Fig. 4–10 Contour Fixture Assembly

piece of lumber $1\frac{5}{8}$ inch square and is adjustable in height to accept any thickness of chair blank between $\frac{3}{32}$ and $\frac{1}{4}$ inch. For best results, the contour depth should not exceed one-third of the blank thickness.

The other tool is the router bit, a Dremel #H66, with a $\frac{1}{4}$ inch diameter teardrop-shaped cutter and a $\frac{1}{8}$ inch diameter shank. Because the shank diameter is used as a guide for the width of the contour outline, using a different cutter will require altering the fixture dimensions.

CUTTING CONTOUR ON SEAT
BLANK

Cut seat blank to size and insert between top and base of fixture. Then tighten nuts on bolts. Place assembly on drill stand to adjust for depth of contour cut, identified as X in Fig. 4–11. (See Fig. 4–12 for typical setup.) For safety, disconnect drill from power supply before attempting to adjust drill stand to desired

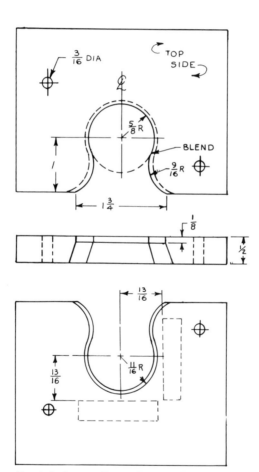

Fig. 4–9 Contour Fixture Top Detail

24

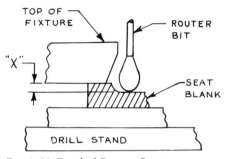

Fig. 4-11 Detail of Contour Setup

height. When proper height has been set, lock drill and drill stand in position. With power on, move fixture across top of drill stand to engage router. Then follow the template contour with router

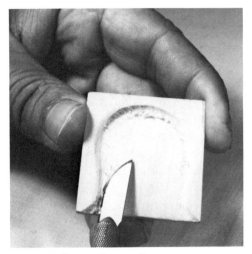

Fig. 4-13 Shaping Contour Seat

Fig. 4-12 Drill and Contour Fixture Assembly

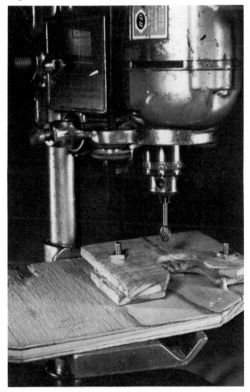

shank. Remove blank from fixture and check for symmetrical pattern on seat blank. Adjust guides on fixture as required, and attach permanently. If desired, a second cut may be made inside the first to reduce the amount of knife work necessary to finish seat contour.

Fig. 4-14 Finished Contour Seat

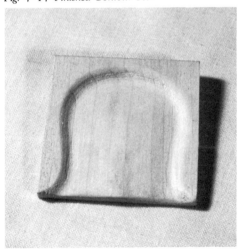

Remove the chair blank from fixture, and shape seat contour with a curved knife blade (Fig. 4–13). Drill required holes prior to rounding corners. Then sand with extra-fine sandpaper to remove knife blade and router bit marks. (See Fig. 4–14 for finished seat contour.)

The depth of the cut may be varied from front to back by adding several layers of masking tape at the back on the underside of the chair blank before inserting into the fixture. This will produce a shallow cut in the front and gradually increase in depth toward the back. Experiment with different layers of tape until you find the desired effect.

A suggestion: Cut and contour several blanks at one time to make matched pairs or to replace one where the knife cut was too deep.

CANING CHAIR SEATS

The caning material used on the ladder-back chair and the woodcarver's chair is crochet thread, size A 65. Select beige, ecru, or pale yellow. Avoid pure white because it is easily soiled.

For a very neat, square, cane pattern, keep the variation in length of the seat stringers to a minimum. Slight variations in length can be compensated for by adding an additional strand or two to

Fig. 4–15 Caning Shuttle

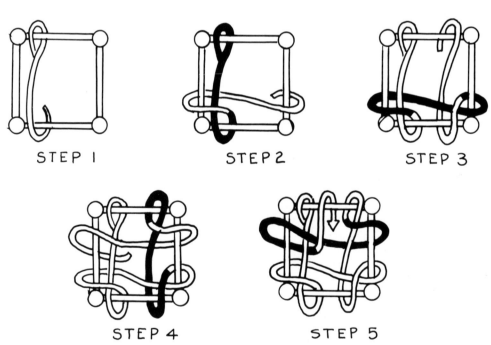

STEP 1 STEP 2 STEP 3

STEP 4 STEP 5

Fig. 4–16 Pattern for Caning Chair Seat

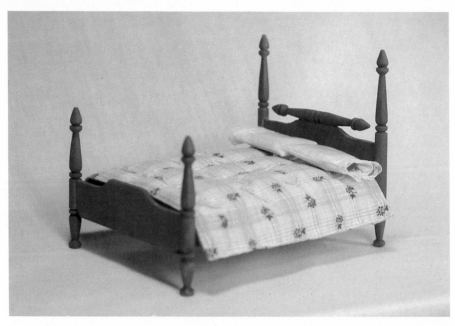

center the pattern. Extreme variations in the length of the stringers should be avoided because the chair will not be square.

A caning shuttle is a helpful tool in handling the twelve to fifteen feet of crochet thread necessary for each chair. Shorter lengths can be handled with a needle, but the knots detract from the appearance even if they are under the chair seat. The shuttle (Fig. 4–15) was fashioned from a large paper clip; any wire about 6½ inches long and $\frac{1}{16}$ inch in diameter is fine. Straighten wire, and then form as shown.

Begin by wrapping twelve feet of crochet thread between the hooks of the shuttle. Start caning by attaching a loop

Fig. 4–17 Caning Chair

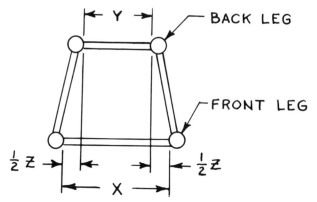

Fig. 4–18 Trapezoidal-Shaped Chair Seat

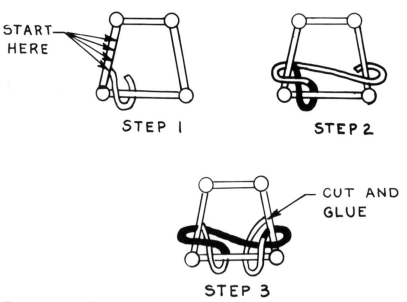

Fig. 4–19 Caning Pattern for Trapezoidal Chair

of thread to the stringer on the back of the chair, either by tieing a knot or gluing the loop end. Then proceed with steps 1 through 5 (Fig. 4–16). Pull thread snug but not tight. Repeat steps 1 through 5 until chair is completed. (Refer to Fig. 4–17.) If the pattern appears off center, continue with additional strands to center pattern or compress the rows on the long side and loosen the rows on the short side.

CANING CHAIRS WITH TRAPEZOIDAL SEATS

The Woodcarver's chair (Fig. 6–39) has a trapezoidal seat—wider in front than in back. This type of chair cannot be caned by the usual method. The difference in width between the front legs and back legs will have to be measured to determine the amount of caning required

to "square" the seat pattern. (Refer to Fig. 4–18.) Measure the distance between front legs (X), subtract the distance between the back legs (Y), and then divide the answer (Z) by 2. (i.e. $X - Y = Z \div 2 = \frac{1}{2}Z$). This equals the amount of offset on one side of the chair, between the back and the front legs. The number of strands of thread required to cover the offset ($\frac{1}{2}Z$) will "square" the seat pattern.

Start caning by attaching thread (Fig. 4–19). Then proceed with steps 1, 2, and 3. Cut thread and glue to opposite side. Then repeat steps 1, 2, and 3 until the required number of strands have been added to "square" the seat pattern. Then revert to the regular caning method (Fig. 4–16), and complete the caning of the chair. Additional strands may be required to center the caned pattern.

CHAPTER 5

Kitchen Group

The various furniture pieces that comprise the kitchen group are shown in Figs. 5–1, 5–2, and 5–3. All of these pieces are built from the individual plans outlined on the following pages.

TRESTLE TABLE

A trestle table is an extremely durable piece of furniture that is constructed without the use of nails or screws. Many original Early American pieces were produced in just this manner. The table tops are made by pegging several boards together; the top is then pegged to the legs. The crossbrace, with mortise and tenon construction, adds extra rigidity to the legs. The bench for the trestle table is constructed in the same manner.

The plans for the trestle table (Fig. 5–4) are detailed below.

MATERIALS

PART		DIMENSIONS	QUANTITY
A	Top	$\frac{1}{8} \times 3 \times 6$	1
B	Leg	$\frac{1}{8} \times 2\frac{3}{4} \times 2\frac{3}{8}$	2
C	Brace	$\frac{3}{16} \times \frac{3}{8} \times 4\frac{3}{4}$	1
D	Support	$\frac{3}{32} \times \frac{1}{4} \times 1\frac{7}{8}$	2
E	Peg	$\frac{1}{8} \times \frac{1}{8} \times \frac{3}{4}$	2

CONSTRUCTION

1. Cut top **A** to pattern (Fig. 5–5). Then round top edges and corners with fine grade sandpaper.
2. Cut leg **B** to pattern (Fig. 5–5). For ease in duplicating the pattern, use masking tape to hold the two pieces together while cutting pattern with coping saw

Fig. 5–1 Kitchen Furniture Group: Trestle Table, Ladder-Back Chairs, and Accessories

Fig. 5–2 Kitchen Furniture Group: Hutch, Dough Box, Ladder-Back Chair, and Accessories

Fig. 5–3 Kitchen Furniture Group: Sugar Bin, Dough Box, Chair Table, Ladder-Back Chair

or jigsaw. To cut mortise hole in legs, first drill a $\frac{1}{8}$ inch hole and then shape with a knife to accept the tenon of the crossbrace. Sand edges of legs with sandpaper wrapped around a dowel.

3. Cut brace **C** to length, and complete brace detail (Fig. 5–6).

4. Cut support **D** to pattern (Fig. 5–5).

Fig. 5–4 Trestle Table and Benches

5. Cut pegs **E** to length, and then taper to $\frac{3}{32}$ diameter.

6. Sandpaper parts in direction of wood grain, and then stain to desired color. To prevent top from warping, apply a weight to top after staining and allow to dry.

ASSEMBLY

1. Dry fit legs, crossbrace, and pegs together **B**, **C**, and **E**. After obtaining a satisfactory fit, disassemble, apply glue to the joints, and reassemble (Fig. 5–7).

2. Glue one support **D** to the inside of each leg, item **B**, centered and flush with the top of each leg.

3. Attach top **A** with glue, centered and square, to the legs. Apply a weight or clamp to assembly until the glue has dried.

4. When glue has dried, apply finish coat

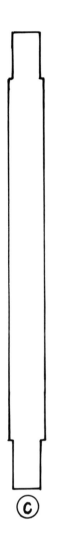

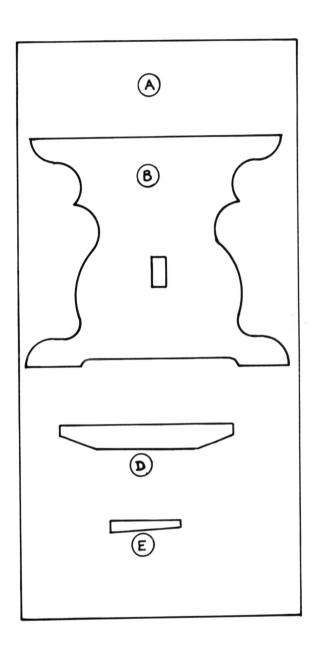

Fig. 5–5 Pattern for Trestle Table

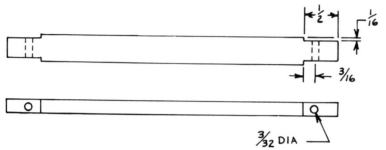

Fig. 5–6 Detail of Crossbar

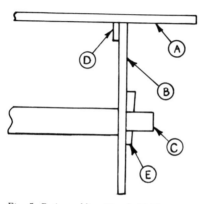

Fig. 5–7 Assembling Trestle Table

of spray varnish. Buff lightly with steel wool and apply second coat if desired.

TRESTLE TABLE BENCHES

The trestle table benches are assembled in the same manner as the trestle table.

MATERIALS

PART		DIMENSIONS	QUANTITY
A	Seat	$\frac{1}{8} \times 1 \times 5$	1
B	Leg	$\frac{1}{8} \times \frac{15}{16} \times 1\frac{7}{8}$	2
C	Brace	$\frac{1}{8} \times \frac{1}{4} \times 4\frac{1}{2}$	1
D	Peg	$\frac{3}{32} \times \frac{3}{32} \times \frac{3}{8}$	2

CONSTRUCTION

1. Cut seat **A** to size. Then round corners and top edges with fine sandpaper.
2. Cut legs **B** (Fig. 5–8), with jigsaw. To cut mortise hole in legs, first drill a $\frac{3}{32}$ inch diameter hole, then shape with knife to accept tenon of brace. Sand edges with sandpaper wrapped around a dowel.
3. Cut brace **C** to length and complete brace detail (Fig. 5–9).
4. Cut peg **D** to length, and taper to $\frac{1}{16}$ inch diameter.
5. Sandpaper parts in direction of wood grain, and stain to match trestle table color.

ASSEMBLY

1. Dry fit legs, brace, and pegs **B**, **C**, and **D** together for proper fit. Then disassemble, apply glue to the joints, and reassemble in the same manner as the trestle table (Fig. 5–7).
2. Center and square seat **A** with legs and attach with glue. Apply a weight or clamp until the glue dries.
3. When the glue has dried, apply a light coat of satin finish polyurethane. Buff lightly with steel wool and apply second coat if desired.

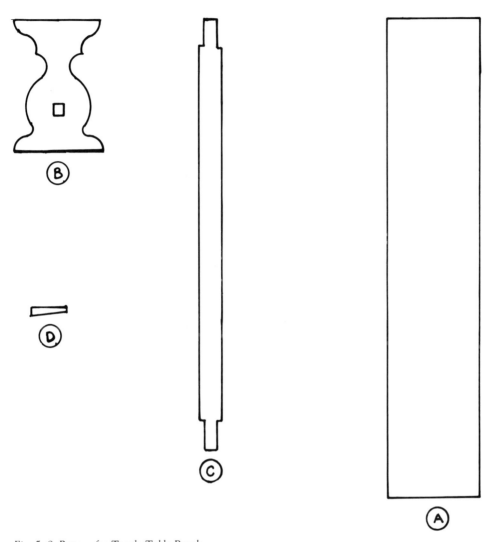

Fig. 5–8 Pattern for Trestle Table Bench

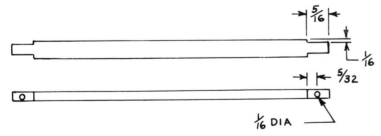

Fig. 5–9 Detail of Bench Brace

Fig. 5–10 Chair Table

CHAIR TABLE

The chair table (Fig. 5–10) as the name implies, was designed as a dual-purpose piece of furniture. It could be converted into either a chair or a table simply by removing the wooden pegs that held the top in place. In its day, it was a very functional piece of furniture; it required less lumber to build and, once built, it took up less space than the two pieces of furniture it replaced. The drawer located below the seat served as a knife holder or sewing box, depending on its location in the home.

MATERIALS

PART		DIMENSIONS	QUANTITY
A	Top	$\frac{3}{32} \times 3\frac{3}{8}$ diameter	1
B	Leg	$\frac{1}{8} \times 1\frac{1}{2} \times 2\frac{1}{4}$	2
C	Seat	$\frac{3}{32} \times 1\frac{3}{8} \times 2$	1
D	Support	$\frac{3}{32} \times 1\frac{3}{16} \times 2$	1
E	Back	$\frac{1}{16} \times 1\frac{5}{16} \times 2$	1
F	Base	$\frac{3}{32} \times \frac{1}{4} \times 1\frac{11}{16}$	2
G	Strut	$\frac{3}{32} \times \frac{1}{4} \times 1\frac{1}{2}$	2
H	Peg	$\frac{3}{32}$ dia. $\times \frac{3}{8}$ long	4
I	Drawer Front	$\frac{3}{32} \times \frac{7}{16} \times 1\frac{15}{16}$	1
J	Drawer Bottom	$\frac{1}{32} \times 1 \times 1\frac{7}{8}$	1
K	Drawer Side	$\frac{1}{32} \times \frac{9}{32} \times 1$	2
L	Drawer Back	$\frac{1}{32} \times \frac{9}{32} \times 1\frac{7}{8}$	1
M	Drawer Pull	(purchased)	1

CONSTRUCTION

1. With a jigsaw, cut top **A** to pattern (Fig. 5–11).
2. Cut and drill two legs **B** to pattern (Fig. 5–12).
3. Cut and drill strut **G** to pattern (Fig. 5–13).
4. Cut peg **H** to length and reduce one end to fit a $\frac{1}{16}$ inch diameter hole loosely (Fig. 5–11).
5. Cut remaining pieces to dimensions indicated.
6. Sandpaper all parts in direction of wood grain, and stain to desired color.

ASSEMBLY

1. For assembling base, refer to Fig. 5–14. Center bases, **F** on bottom of legs **B** and glue in place.
2. Install back **E** flush with back of legs. This will locate position of seat **C** at the $1\frac{1}{2}$ inch height.

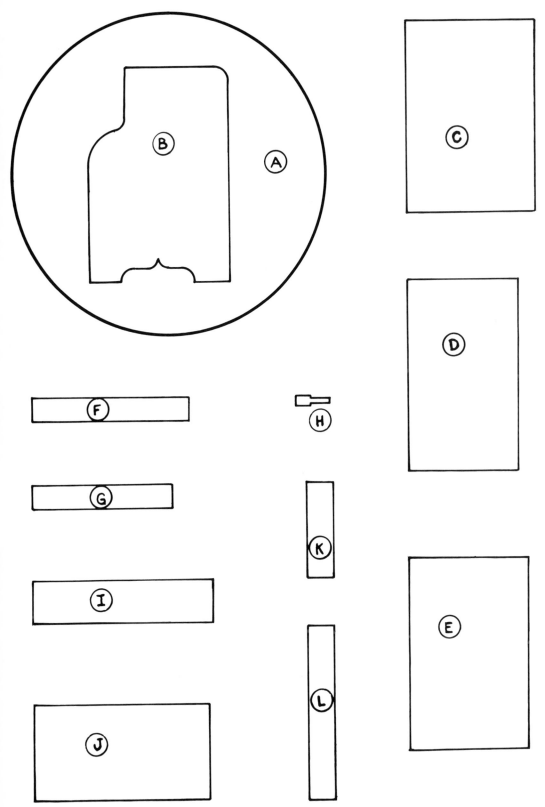

Fig. 5–11 Pattern for Chair Table

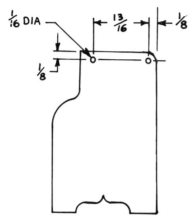

Fig. 5–12 *Detail of Chair Table Leg*

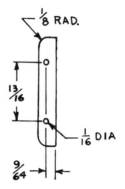

Fig. 5–13 *Detail of Chair Table Strut*

3. Locate support **D** $\frac{3}{8}$ inch below seat (Fig. 5–14). Attach a wide rubber band around assembly as a glue clamp.

4. Assemble struts **G** to underside of top **A** with glue, $2\frac{5}{16}$ inch apart and centered.

5. When glue has dried, attach top to base assembly with pegs **H** (Fig. 5–15).

6. Assemble drawer pieces **I**, **J**, **K**, and **L** (Figs. 5–16 and 5–17) with sides flush to top of drawer front.

7. Place drawer in position and apply a

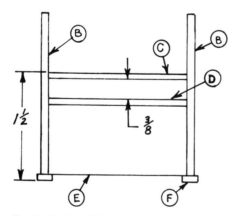

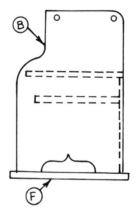

Fig. 5–14 *Assembling Chair Table Base*

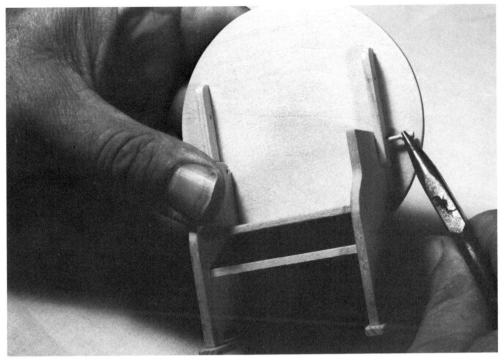

Fig. 5–15 Installing Chair Table Hinge

light finish coat of semigloss polyurethane.

8. When finish is dry, attach drawer pull
M to center of drawer with miniature
nails or shortened pins.

Fig. 5–17 Assembling Chair Table Drawer

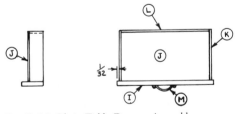

Fig. 5–16 Chair Table Drawer Assembly

SUGAR BIN

The sugar bin (Fig. 5–18) is a replica of a bygone era. As the name implies, it was used as a storage place for a large quantity of sugar, usually the family's winter supply, which might have been 100 pounds or more. The drawers on the top were used to store a variety of things, including spices, knives, and an assortment of kitchen utensils.

Fig. 5–18 Sugar Bin

MATERIALS

PART		DIMENSIONS	QUANTITY
A	Top	$\frac{3}{16} \times 1\frac{3}{16} \times 3$	1
B	Side	$\frac{3}{16} \times 1\frac{5}{8} \times 2\frac{7}{16}$	2
C	Shelf	$\frac{3}{16} \times \frac{15}{16} \times 2\frac{3}{8}$	3
D	Back	$\frac{1}{16} \times 2\frac{7}{16} \times 2\frac{3}{8}$	1
E	Brace	$\frac{3}{32} \times \frac{5}{16} \times 2\frac{3}{4}$	1
F	Lid	$\frac{3}{32} \times \frac{5}{8} \times 2\frac{3}{4}$	1
G	Front	$\frac{1}{16} \times \frac{15}{16} \times 2\frac{3}{4}$	1
H	Base Side	$\frac{1}{16} \times \frac{7}{16} \times 1$	2
I	Base Front	$\frac{1}{16} \times \frac{7}{16} \times 2\frac{7}{8}$	1
J	Drawer Front	$\frac{3}{32} \times \frac{5}{8} \times 2\frac{1}{2}$	1
K	Drawer Back	$\frac{3}{32} \times \frac{1}{2} \times 2\frac{1}{8}$	1
L	Drawer Side	$\frac{3}{32} \times \frac{1}{2} \times \frac{7}{8}$	2
M	Drawer Bottom	$\frac{3}{32} \times \frac{25}{32} \times 2\frac{1}{8}$	1
N	Hinge	$\frac{1}{8} \times \frac{7}{16}$ masking tape	2
	Knobs	Lacing beads and nails	4

CONSTRUCTION

1. Cut side **B** to pattern (Fig. 5–19).
2. Cut base trim **I** to pattern (Fig. 5–19).
3. Cut drawer front **J** to dimension. Then cut grooves (Fig. 5–24).
4. Cut remaining pieces to dimension, noting that **E** and **G** will have to be modified when assembled.
5. Cut hinge **N**, from masking tape to diamond shape (Fig. 5–19). Then paint hinges with flat black paint.
6. Sand and stain parts to desired color.

ASSEMBLY

1. Glue the three shelves **C** flush with the front of sides **B** and located as indicated in (Fig. 5–20).
2. Glue back **D** flush with back of legs at top and bottom.
3. Glue top **A** centered between legs and flush with back.
4. Refer to Fig. 5–21. Bevel edge of brace **E** to fit flush with center shelf and sides. Then glue in position.
5. Bevel edge of front **G** to fit flush with bottom shelf and sides.
6. Glue base sides **H** flush with back of leg as shown, one on each end.
7. Glue base front **I** flush with edges and bottom of legs as shown.

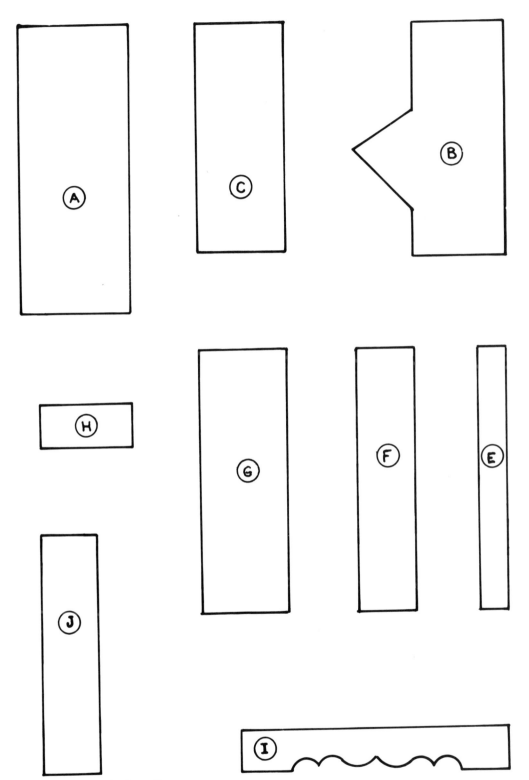

Fig. 5–19 Pattern for Sugar Bin

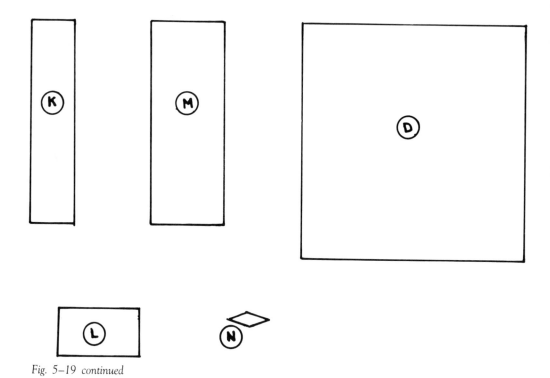

Fig. 5–19 continued

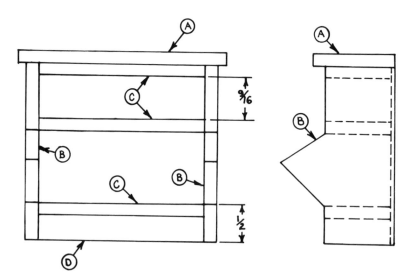

Fig. 5–20 Assembling Sugar Bin Base

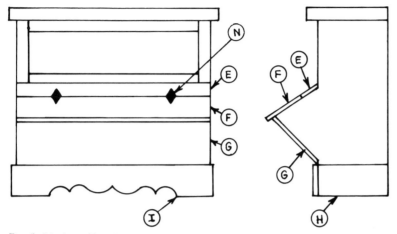

Fig. 5–21 Assembling Sugar Bin

Fig. 5–22 Installing Hinges on Sugar Bin

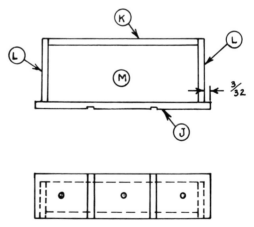

Fig. 5–23 Sugar Bin Drawer Assembly

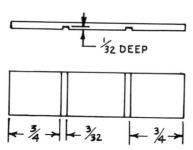

Fig. 5–24 *Detail of Drawer Front*

$\frac{1}{32}$ DEEP

$\frac{3}{4}$ $\frac{3}{32}$ $\frac{3}{4}$

Fig. 5–25 *Dough Box*

8. Attach lid **F** to brace **E** with hinges **N**, glue in position (Figs. 5–21 and 5–22).

9. Attach drawer parts, sides, bottom, and back **K**, **L**, and **M** with glue to drawer front **J** (Fig. 5–23), flush and centered to drawer front.

10. Apply a light coat of finish to assembly. Then slide drawer and lid to prevent sticking.

11. When finish has dried, attach three knobs (lacing bead and nail) to drawer front and one knob to center of lid.

DOUGH BOX

The dough box (Fig. 5–25) contained the colonial family's flour supply. The dough for making bread was blended and kneaded and then placed in the dough box before baking to permit the dough to rise. For that reason, the dough box was always placed close to a wood-burning stove to maintain the warmth required to activate the yeast in the dough. Many variations of the dough box survive; some have legs that are ornately carved, others are turned on a wood lathe. The size of the box was generally established by the size of the family.

MATERIALS

PART		DIMENSIONS	QUANTITY
A	Leg	$\frac{1}{4} \times \frac{1}{4} \times \frac{3}{4}$	4
B	Side	$\frac{3}{32} \times 1\frac{1}{4} \times 1\frac{3}{4}$	2
C	End	$\frac{3}{32} \times 1\frac{1}{4} \times 1\frac{1}{8}$	2
D	Base	$\frac{1}{8} \times 1\frac{3}{8} \times 1\frac{7}{8}$	1
E	Top	$\frac{3}{32} \times 1 \times 1\frac{1}{2}$	2
F	Hinge	$\frac{1}{8} \times \frac{7}{16}$ masking tape	2

CONSTRUCTION

1. Cut base **D** and top **E** to dimensions and pattern (Fig. 5–26).

2. To shape legs **A** cut four pieces of $\frac{1}{4}$ inch square material about 1 inch long, with a 10° compound angle cut on one end (Fig. 5–27). Then cut leg to $\frac{3}{4}$ inch length and shape base of leg as shown, using a sharp knife.

3. Cut hinges **F** from masking tape or thin leather to the diamond shape shown in the pattern (Fig. 5–26).

4. The two sides **B** and the two ends **C** require a 5° angle cut at the top edge

44

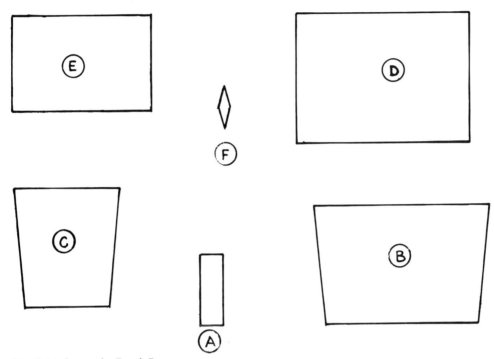

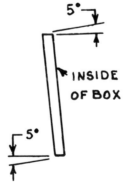

Fig. 5–26 Pattern for Dough Box

and a 5° parallel cut on the bottom edge (Fig. 5–28).

5. Sand parts, and stain to desired color.

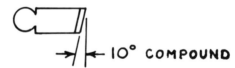

Fig. 5–27 Detail of Dough Box Leg

ASSEMBLY

1. Dry assemble sides, ends, and base **B**, **C** and **D**. Remove the vertical gap that appears between the ends and the sides by lightly sanding the end piece. Then glue in position and assemble (Fig. 5–29).

2. Center top pieces **E** on box and glue *one* piece in place. Position other top piece and glue hinges **F** in place.

3. Invert assembly and glue legs **A** in place, so that all legs are tilted outward in both directions (Fig. 5–29).

4. Apply a light coat of spray satin finish.

Fig. 5–28 Detail for Cutting Ends and Sides

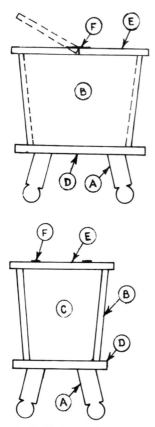

Fig. 5–29 Assembling Dough Box

LADDER-BACK CHAIR

The ladder-back chair (Fig. 5–30) not only is a functional piece of furniture but an attractive one also. This chair is a simple, lightweight piece that is extremely strong and durable.

Two plans for this chair are offered. The first chair (not shown) requires very little shaping; it was included for that reason. The second chair (Fig. 5–30) follows the complete hole pattern of the first chair but requires considerable shaping of the spindle legs. The backs of these chairs sometimes were painted or

carved with various leaf patterns. The second chair (Fig. 5–31) was painted flat black; then the eagle wings were painted in antique gold hobby paint. The method for caning these chairs is found in Chapter 4.

MATERIALS

PART		DIMENSIONS	QUANTITY
A	Back Leg	$\frac{5}{32}$ dia. dowel $\times$ $3\frac{1}{2}$	2
B	Front Leg	$\frac{5}{32}$ dia. dowel $\times$ $1\frac{5}{8}$	2
C	Rung	$\frac{3}{32}$ dia. dowel $\times$ $1\frac{7}{16}$	8
D	Back	$\frac{1}{16} \times \frac{1}{4} \times 1\frac{7}{16}$	4

Fig. 5–30 Ladder-Back Chair

Fig. 5–31 Painted Ladder-Back Chair

CONSTRUCTION

1. Refer to Fig. 5–32 for the chair pattern.
2. Cut back legs **A** to length. Then shape and drill holes $\frac{1}{16}$ inch deep, following pattern (Fig. 5–33).
3. Remove the four webs between holes located $\frac{1}{8}$ inch apart (Fig. 5–34). This will form the mortise hole for the back tenon to fit into.
4. To shape the back pieces **D** tape four pieces together and cut on a jigsaw to pattern (Fig. 5–35).
5. Shape eight rungs **C** (Fig. 5–36). Make the $1\frac{5}{16}$ inch dimension as accurately as possible, for this affects the squareness of the chair and later will affect the caned seat pattern.
6. Cut front legs **B** to length and drill hole pattern $\frac{1}{16}$ inch deep (Fig. 5–37).
7. Sand parts lightly with fine sandpaper.
8. Parts may be stained or left natural.

ASSEMBLY

1. After checking for proper fit, glue the four back pieces **D**, and two rungs **C** to the two back legs **A** in respective positions (Fig. 5–38). Use a clamp or rub-

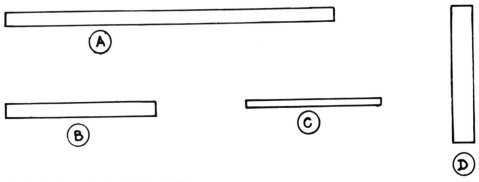

Fig. 5–32 Pattern for Ladder-Back Chair

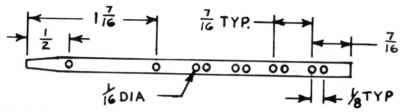

Fig. 5–33 Detail of Ladder-Back Chair Leg

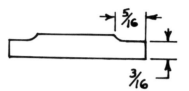

Fig. 5–35 Detail of Back for Ladder-Back Chair

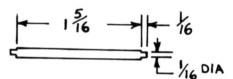

Fig. 5–36 Detail of Rung for Ladder-Back Chair

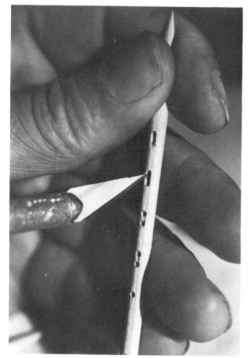

Fig. 5–34 Detail of Removing Web between Holes

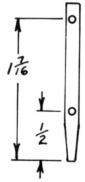

Fig. 5–37 Detail of Front Leg for Ladder-Back Chair

ber bands to hold legs parallel while glue is drying.

2. Attach two rungs **C** to the hole pattern of front legs **B** with glue.

3. Drill hole pattern (Fig. 5–38) to match both front legs with both back legs.

4. Attach remaining four rungs **C** between front and back legs. After checking for squareness, glue four rungs in place. Hold chair legs in squared position while glue is drying.

5. Refer to Chapter 4 for caning details.

LADDER-BACK CHAIR 2

A different ladder-back chair can be made using the same materials list, dimensions, and hole patterns as the first chair. This chair has more detail on the front and back legs than the previous chair.

CONSTRUCTION

1. Use the materials list for the previous ladder-back chair.

2. Cut piece parts to pattern (Fig. 5–32).

3. Drill hole pattern in back legs (Fig. 5–33).

4. Shape back panels (Fig. 5–35).

5. Detail rungs (Fig. 5–36).

6. Drill hole pattern in front legs (Fig. 5–37).

7. Shape front and back legs to pattern (Fig. 5–39).

ASSEMBLY

Refer to assembly detail for the previous chair and follow instructions.

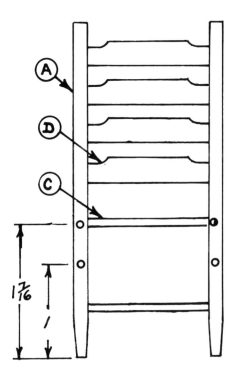

Fig. 5–38 Assembling Ladder-Back Chair

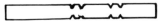

Fig. 5–39 Pattern for Ladder-Back Chair #2

HUTCH

The Hutch (Fig. 5–40) may be used in either the kitchen or the dining room. The units designed for the dining room generally had doors on the upper part rather than exposed shelves and small drawers; these were usually of a later period than the unit shown here. Recent modifications have added glass to the door panels; these are typically dining room furniture.

Because of its complex construction, the hutch is described here as two separate units, the base and the top. The base unit alone is a storage cabinet (Fig. 5–41). The top may be either glued to the base or left unattached.

MATERIALS

PART		DIMENSIONS	QUANTITY
A	Leg	$\frac{1}{8} \times 1\frac{1}{2} \times 2\frac{13}{16}$	2
B	Drawer Guide	$\frac{3}{16} \times 1\frac{7}{16} \times 2\frac{13}{16}$	1
C	Bottom Shelf	$\frac{1}{8} \times 1\frac{7}{16} \times 2\frac{13}{16}$	1
D	Support	$\frac{1}{8} \times 1\frac{7}{16} \times 2\frac{13}{16}$	1
E	Divider	$\frac{1}{16} \times \frac{5}{16} \times 2\frac{13}{16}$	1
F	Center Shelf	$\frac{3}{32} \times 1\frac{3}{16} \times 2\frac{13}{16}$	1
G	Top	$\frac{3}{16} \times 1\frac{5}{8} \times 3\frac{1}{4}$	1
H	Back	$\frac{1}{16} \times 2\frac{13}{16} \times 2\frac{13}{16}$	1
I	Base Front	$\frac{1}{16} \times \frac{5}{16} \times 3\frac{3}{16}$	1
J	Base Side	$\frac{1}{16} \times \frac{5}{16} \times 1\frac{1}{2}$	2

(The following materials are for the door detail; 2 required)

K	Frame Top and Bottom	$\frac{1}{8} \times \frac{3}{16} \times 1\frac{7}{32}$	2
L	Frame Side	$\frac{1}{8} \times \frac{3}{16} \times 1\frac{1}{4}$	2

M	Panel	$\frac{3}{32} \times \frac{5}{8} \times 1\frac{1}{16}$	1
N	Back	$\frac{1}{32} \times 1\frac{7}{32} \times 1\frac{5}{8}$	1

(The following materials are for the drawer detail; 2 required)

O	Drawer Front	$\frac{1}{16} \times \frac{1}{2} \times 1\frac{5}{16}$	1
P	Drawer Bottom	$\frac{1}{16} \times 1\frac{3}{16} \times 1\frac{7}{16}$	1
Q	Drawer Side	$\frac{1}{32} \times \frac{5}{16} \times 1\frac{3}{16}$	2
R	Drawer Back	$\frac{1}{32} \times \frac{5}{16} \times 1\frac{5}{32}$	1

Fig. 5–40 Hutch Assembly

Fig. 5–41 Hutch Base Assembly

CONSTRUCTION (BASE)

1. Cut front base **I** to configuration shown in the pattern layout (Fig. 5–42).
2. Cut drawer guide, bottom shelf, and support **B**, **C**, and **D** to dimensions indicated. Then add notch (Fig. 5–43), but drill holes for door hinges in **B** and **C** only.
3. Cut remaining parts to size and shape indicated.
4. Sand parts lightly and stain all parts to desired color.

ASSEMBLY

1. Assemble back **H** to the inside of legs **A** flush at top, bottom, and back edges of the legs with glue. See assembly detail (Fig. 5–44).
2. Glue support **D** and bottom shelf **C**, flush with front edges of legs and against back, at dimensions indicated.

3. Insert drawer guide **B** to dimension with glue, flush with front edges of legs and against back.
4. Glue center shelf **F** against back at the dimensions indicated.
5. Glue vertical divider **E** in place, flush with topside of support **D**.
6. Glue top **G** flush with back, centered and square with legs.
7. Attach large rubber bands over the top and around the legs to clamp base while the glue is drying.

CONSTRUCTION (DOORS)

1. Cut frames and back **K**, **L**, and **N** to dimensions specified.
2. Cut panel **M** to size. Then bevel front edges at 45° by sanding with fine sandpaper.
3. Sand and stain parts to match the hutch base color.

ASSEMBLY

1. Glue frame members **K** and **L** flush with outside edge of back **N** and butted flush against each other (Fig. 5–45).
2. Center panel **M** and glue in place.
3. Match door to base assembly (adjust fit if necessary) centered in door cavity.
4. Install a short length of #24 AWG copper into the previously drilled holes of drawer guide and bottom shelf (Fig. 5–46). Press wire $\frac{1}{16}$ inch deep into door, and trim wire flush.
5. Attach doorknobs of your choice.

CONSTRUCTION (DRAWERS)

1. Cut drawer front, bottom, sides, and back **O**, **P**, **Q**, and **R** to dimensions indicated.
2. Sand and stain to match color of hutch base.

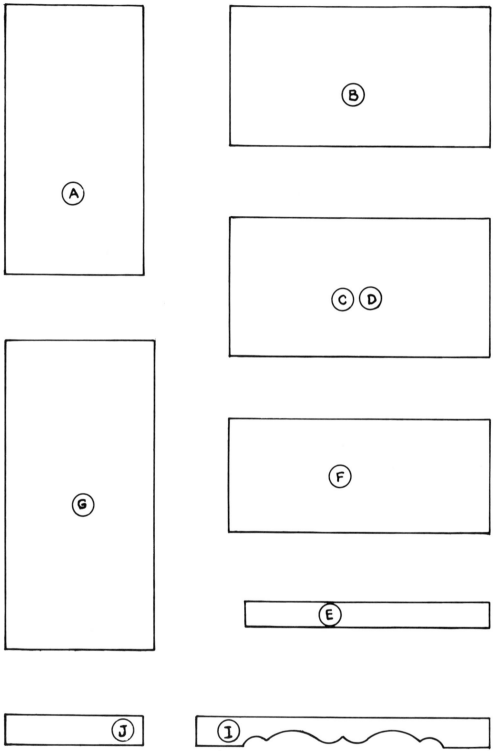

Fig. 5–42 Pattern for Hutch Base

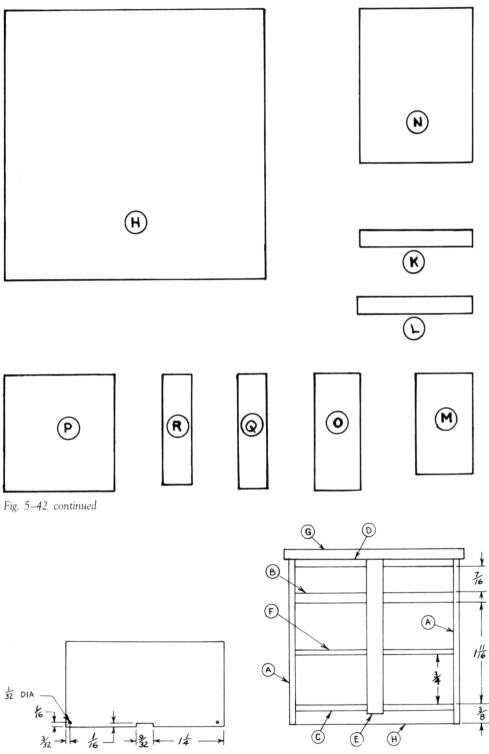

Fig. 5-42 continued

Fig. 5-43 Detail of Drawer Guide and Shelf

Fig. 5-44 Assembling Hutch Base

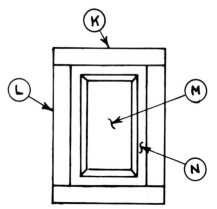

Fig. 5–45 Assembling Hutch Door

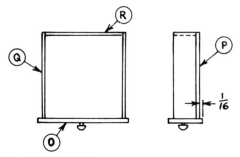

Fig. 5–47 Hutch Drawer Assembly

ASSEMBLY

1. Assemble drawer pieces **O**, **P**, **Q**, and **R** (Fig. 5–47) with glue. They were dimensioned to assure a snug fit; if too snug, sand lightly on sides and bottom.
2. Attach knobs to center of each drawer and install in hutch base.

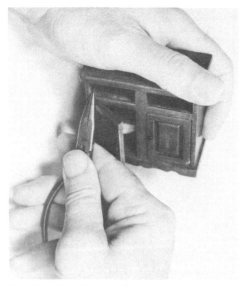

Fig. 5–46 Installing Hutch Hinge Pin

3. Apply a light coat of finish to base assembly. Open doors and drawers to prevent sticking.
4. Buff lightly with steel wool, and apply a second coat if desired.

MATERIALS (TOP)

PART		DIMENSIONS	QUANTITY
A	Side	$\frac{1}{8} \times \frac{3}{4} \times 2\frac{7}{8}$	2
B	Top Shelf	$\frac{3}{32} \times \frac{11}{16} \times 2\frac{13}{16}$	1
C	Bottom Guide	$\frac{3}{32} \times \frac{3}{4} \times 2\frac{13}{16}$	1
D	Back	$\frac{1}{16} \times 1\frac{7}{8} \times 2\frac{13}{16}$	1
E	Top Guide	$\frac{3}{32} \times \frac{11}{16} \times 2\frac{13}{16}$	1
F	Drawer Spacer	$\frac{1}{16} \times \frac{3}{8} \times \frac{11}{16}$	3
G	Drawer Front	$\frac{1}{16} \times \frac{11}{32} \times \frac{5}{8}$	1*
H	Drawer Side	$\frac{1}{32} \times \frac{5}{16} \times \frac{5}{8}$	2*
I	Drawer Back	$\frac{1}{32} \times \frac{5}{16} \times \frac{9}{16}$	1*
J	Drawer Bottom	$\frac{1}{32} \times \frac{5}{8} \times \frac{5}{8}$	1*

*Quantity required for each drawer.

CONSTRUCTION

1. For the sides **A** trace pattern (Fig. 5–48) on one board. Then tape two pieces together and cut out pattern with jig-

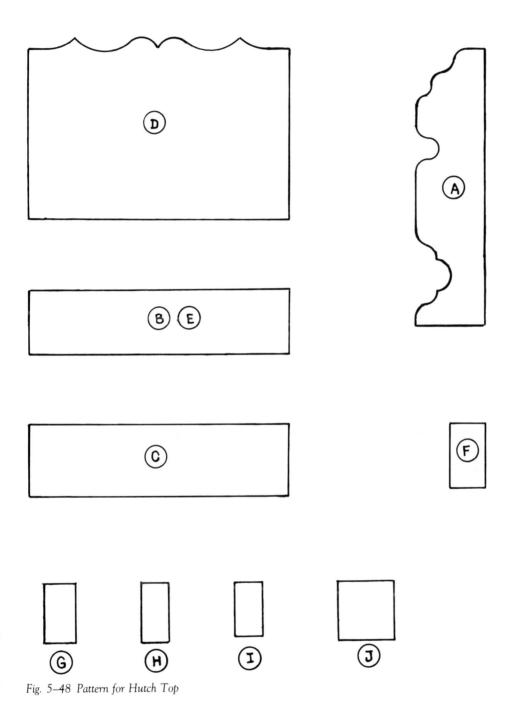

Fig. 5–48 Pattern for Hutch Top

saw. To maintain duplication of pattern, use fine sandpaper wrapped around a piece of doweling and sand edges while the two pieces are still taped together.

2. Cut back **D** to pattern (Fig. 5–48).
3. Cut required quantities of remaining pieces **B**, **C**, **E**, and **F** to dimensions indicated.
4. Sand lightly, and stain to match the color of the hutch base.

ASSEMBLY

1. Glue back **D** flush with top and back of sides **A** (Fig. 5–49).
2. Glue bottom guide **C** flush with bottom of back and flush with front edges of sides.
3. Install top shelf **B** at dimension indicated, against back and flush with front edges of sides.
4. Position drawer spacers **F** at dimensions indicated. Then glue in place flush with front of bottom guide **C**.
5. Glue top guide **E** in position shown, against back and flush with front.
6. Clamp assembly and allow time for glue to dry.

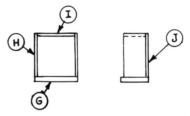

Fig. 5–50 Hutch Top Drawer Assembly

CONSTRUCTION (TOP DRAWERS)

1. Cut drawer parts **G**, **H**, **I**, and **J** to dimensions specified.
2. Sand and stain parts to match color of the hutch top.

ASSEMBLY

1. Glue drawer parts together **G**, **H**, **I** and **J** (Fig. 5–50).
2. The dimensions of the parts will provide a snug fit. If too snug, sand lightly on sides and bottom of drawers, and install drawers in top assembly.
3. Fashion drawer pulls from white lacing beads and gold-colored craft pins. Install one per drawer.
4. Apply a light coat of spray can satin finish. Slide drawers to prevent sticking.

ARMCHAIR

Because the armchair (Fig. 5–51) has a trapezoidal-shaped seat, it will require additional caning to square the seat pattern, as explained in Chapter 4. Place the arms on the chair after the seat has been caned.

MATERIALS

PART		DIMENSIONS	QUANTITY
A	Back Leg	$\frac{5}{32}$ dia. dowel × $3\frac{1}{2}$	2

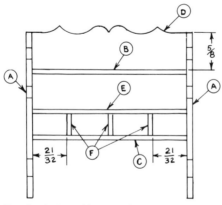

Fig. 5–49 Assembling Hutch Top

Fig. 5–51 Arm Chair

B	*Front Leg*	$\frac{5}{32}$ dia. dowel $\times$ $2\frac{1}{8}$	2
C	*Back*	$\frac{1}{16} \times \frac{3}{8} \times 1\frac{1}{2}$	4
D	*Back Rung*	$\frac{3}{32}$ dia. dowel $\times$ $1\frac{1}{2}$	2
E	*Front Rung*	$\frac{3}{32}$ dia. dowel $\times$ $1\frac{7}{8}$	2
F	*Side Rung*	$\frac{3}{32}$ dia. dowel $\times$ $1\frac{9}{16}$	4
G	*Arm*	$\frac{3}{32} \times \frac{5}{16} \times 1\frac{7}{8}$	2

CONSTRUCTION

1. Cut four backs **C** to pattern (Fig. 5–52).
2. Cut two arms **G** to pattern (Fig. 5–52).
3. Cut two legs **A** to length. Then shape (Fig. 5–53) with a knife. Drill required holes and remove the web between the holes, spaced $\frac{1}{8}$ inch in four places.
4. Cut two front legs **B** to length. Then shape (Fig. 5–54) with a knife. Drill required holes at locations indicated.
5. Cut two back rungs **D** to length. Then shape ends (Fig. 5–55).
6. Cut four side rungs **F** to length. Then shape ends (Fig. 5–55).
7. Cut two front rungs **E** to length. Then shape ends (Fig. 5–55).
8. Sand parts and stain to desired color.

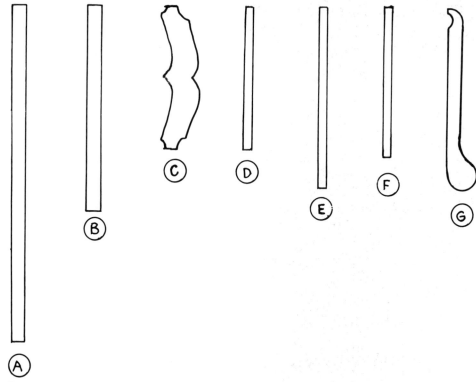

Fig. 5-52 Pattern for Arm Chair

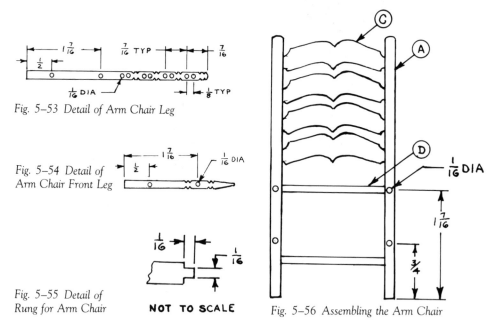

Fig. 5-53 Detail of Arm Chair Leg

Fig. 5-54 Detail of
Arm Chair Front Leg

Fig. 5-55 Detail of
Rung for Arm Chair

NOT TO SCALE

Fig. 5-56 Assembling the Arm Chair

58

ASSEMBLY

1. Attach four backs **C** and two back rungs, item **D**, to back legs **A** with glue (Fig. 5–56). Then drill holes in back leg assembly at locations shown (Fig. 5–56) and angled outward 5°.

2. Attach two front rungs **E** with glue to front legs **B**. Then drill holes in front leg assembly at dimensions shown (Fig. 5–56) and angled inward 5°.

3. Glue two side rungs **F** between each front and back leg **A** and **B**.

4. Refer to Chapter 4 for caning the trapezoidal-shaped seat. When seat has been caned, place arm **G** between front leg and back leg, and glue in place.

CHAPTER 6

Living Room Group

Various arrangements of the individual pieces that constitute the living room group are shown in Figs. 6–1, 6–2, 6–3, and 6–4. This group consists of the cobbler's bench, rocking chair, deacon's bench or settee, desk, captain's chair, woodcarver's chair, and the spinning wheel. You will find various degrees of difficulty building these projects, ranging from the reasonably easy cobbler's bench to the more complicated spinning wheel.

COBBLER'S BENCH

The cobbler's bench was used not only by the local shoemaker, but variations were also used by farmers for repairing harnesses and other leatherwork. Fine

Fig. 6–1 *Living Room Furniture Group: Complete House including Kitchen, Living Room, Den, and Bed Room*

Fig. 6–2 *Living Room Furniture Group: Spinning Wheel, Deacon's Bench, Clock, and Accessories*

Fig. 6–3 *Living Room Furniture Group: Deacon's Bench, Clock, Cobbler's Bench, and Spinning Wheel*

Fig. 6–4 *Living Room Furniture Group: Rocking Chairs, Blanket Chest, Spinning Wheel, and Accessories*

Fig. 6–5 Cobbler's Bench

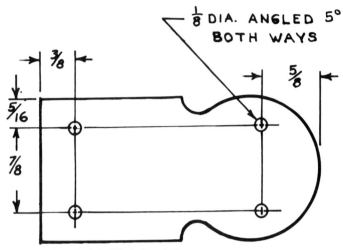

$\frac{1}{8}$ DIA. ANGLED 5°
BOTH WAYS

$\frac{3}{8}$

$\frac{5}{8}$

$\frac{5}{16}$

$\frac{7}{8}$

Fig. 6–7 Detail of Cobbler's Bench Seat

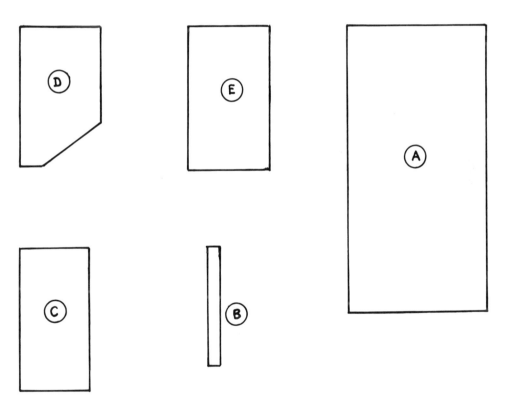

D

E

A

C

B

Fig. 6–6 Pattern for Cobbler's Bench

examples of these antiques exist today. The cobbler's bench (Fig. 6–5) is a memory of a bygone era.

MATERIALS

PART		DIMENSIONS	QUANTITY
A	Seat	$\frac{3}{16} \times 1\frac{1}{2} \times 3$	1
B	Leg	$\frac{5}{32}$ dia. dowel $\times 1\frac{1}{4}$	4
C	Drawers	$\frac{1}{2} \times \frac{3}{4} \times 1\frac{1}{2}$	1
D	Sides	$\frac{3}{32} \times \frac{7}{8} \times 1\frac{7}{16}$	2
E	Back	$\frac{3}{32} \times \frac{7}{8} \times 1\frac{1}{2}$	1

CONSTRUCTION

1. The pattern for the cobbler's bench is shown in Fig. 6–6.
2. Cut pattern for seat **A** (Fig. 6–7) with a coping saw or jigsaw. Shape to contour shown and drill through holes as required.
3. Cut four legs **B** to length, then shape (Fig. 6–8). Refer to Chapter 4 for methods of shaping spindles.
4. Cut drawers **C** to size. Then add saw cuts with hand or table saw (Fig. 6–9).
5. Cut two sides **D** to pattern (Fig. 6–6).
6. Cut back **E** to required dimensions.
7. Sand all parts in direction of wood grain. Then stain to desired color.

ASSEMBLY

1. Dry assemble legs **B** to seat **A** (Fig. 6–10). Legs will protrude through seat and will need to be trimmed flush. Smooth legs and seat with sandpaper. Apply stain to areas requiring it. Re-

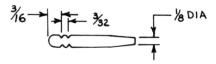

Fig. 6–8 Detail of Cobbler's Bench Leg

64

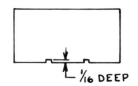

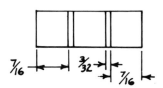

Fig. 6–9 Detail of Cobbler's Bench Drawers

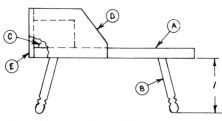

Fig. 6–10 Assembling Cobbler's Bench

move legs, apply glue, and replace legs in respective holes.

2. Glue drawers **C** flush to back edge of seat **A**.
3. Glue back **E** in position shown, flush with edges and bottom of seat.
4. Glue sides **D**, flush with back **E**, and flush with bottom of seat **A**.
5. Cut heads from three craft pins $\frac{1}{4}$ inch long, and insert one in the center of each drawer for a drawer pull.
6. Apply a light coat of satin finish spray varnish, and buff with steel wool.

ROCKING CHAIR

The two rocking chairs shown in Figs. 6–11 and 6–12 are different versions of the same chair. The flat-seated one, which is still produced today, was made as comfortable as possible with the addition of a pad, pillow, or blanket. The contoured seat and curved headrest make the other version more comfortable.

MATERIALS

PART		DIMENSIONS	QUANTITY
A	*Seat*	$\frac{1}{4} \times 1\frac{5}{8} \times 1\frac{5}{8}$	1
B	*Upright*	$\frac{5}{32}$ dia. $\times 1\frac{7}{8}$	2
C	*Leg*	$\frac{5}{32}$ dia. $\times 1\frac{5}{16}$	4
D	*Stretcher*	$\frac{1}{8}$ dia. $\times 1\frac{3}{8}$	3
E	*Spokes*	$\frac{3}{32}$ dia. $\times 1\frac{1}{4}$	3
F	*Back*	$\frac{3}{32} \times \frac{7}{16} \times 1\frac{15}{16}$	1
G	*Arm*	$\frac{1}{8} \times \frac{5}{16} \times 1\frac{11}{16}$	2
H	*Brace 1*	$\frac{1}{8}$ dia. $\times \frac{11}{16}$	2
I	*Brace 2*	$\frac{1}{8}$ dia. $\times \frac{3}{4}$	2
J	*Rocker*	$\frac{1}{8} \times \frac{3}{16} \times 2\frac{5}{8}$	2

Fig. 6–11 Rocking Chair, Flat Seat

Fig. 6–12 Rocking Chair, Contoured Seat

CONSTRUCTION

1. The pattern for the Rocking Chair is shown in Fig. 6–13.
2. Cut seat **A** to size. If seat is to be contoured, refer to Chapter 4 before drilling holes and rounding corners. If flat seat is desired, round corners and drill required hole pattern (Fig. 6–14). Refer to Fig. 6–15 for drilling holes.
3. Cut uprights **B** to length and shape with knife and sandpaper to pattern (Fig. 6–13).
4. Cut legs **C** to length and shape with knife (Fig. 6–13). Drill two $\frac{3}{64}$ inch di-

65

ameter holes at 90° in each front leg and one hole in each back leg.

5. Cut stretcher **D** to length and shape with knife (Fig. 6–13), sizing ends to $\frac{3}{64}$ inch diameter.

6. Cut spokes **E** to length and shape with sandpaper to pattern (Fig. 6–13).

7. Cut back **F** to pattern (Fig. 6–13). Then drill hole pattern (Fig. 6–16). To form back, soak in warm water for ten minutes and shape around paint can with rubber bands until dry.

8. Cut arms **G** to shape (Fig. 6–17). Round top edges with sandpaper and

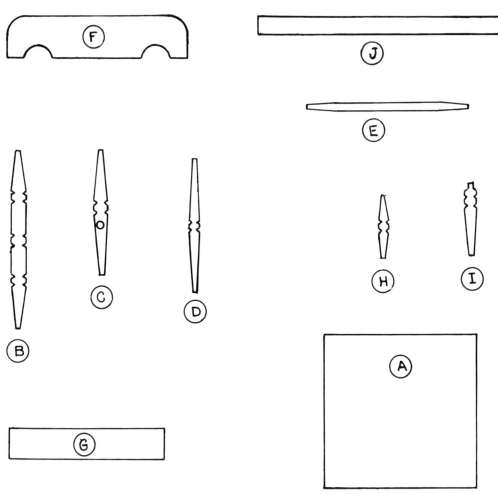

Fig. 6–13 Pattern for Rocking Chair

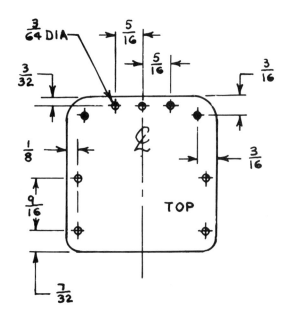

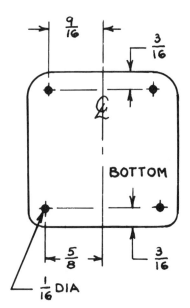

◆ VERTICAL
◆ ANGLED 5°
◆ ANGLED 5° BOTH WAYS

Fig. 6–14 Detail of Rocking Chair Seat

shape end to fit upright. (Additional cutting may be required at assembly.)

9. Cut brace 1 **H** to length and shape with knife (Fig. 6–13).

10. Cut brace 2 **I** to length and shape with knife to pattern (Fig. 6–13).

11. Cut rockers **J** to length. Then bend to shape in same manner as back above.

12. Sand all parts and stain to desired color.

ASSEMBLY

1. Attach stretchers **D** to legs **C** with glue. Then install in bottom of seat **A** (Fig.

6–18). (See Fig. 6–19 for fitting leg to chair seat.)

2. Glue uprights **B** to back **F** (Fig. 6–20). Then glue spokes **E** to back and insert this assembly into seat, item **A**.

3. Place arm braces **H** and **I** on each side of seat and determine hole pattern for arm **G**. Then drill $\frac{3}{64}$ inch diameter holes in arms. Fit arms to braces and uprights and attach with glue.

4. The position of the legs **C** will determine the hole pattern of the rockers **J**. Drill $\frac{3}{64}$ inch diameter holes and attach to legs with glue. Apply weight to seat until glue dries.

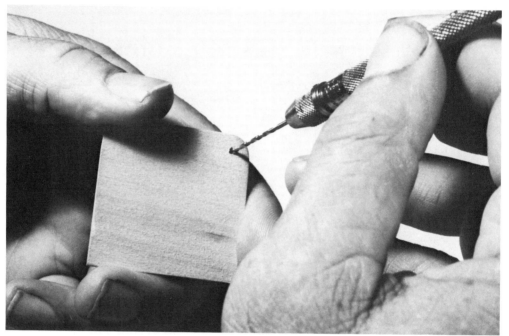

Fig. 6–15 Drilling Holes for Chair Legs

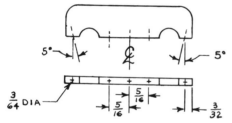

5°   5°

$\frac{3}{64}$ DIA

$\frac{5}{16}$ $\frac{5}{16}$ $\frac{3}{32}$

Fig. 6–16 Detail of Rocking Chair Back

Fig. 6–17 Pattern for Rocking Chair Arm

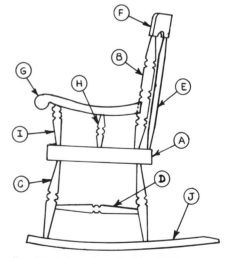

Fig. 6–18 Assembling Rocking Chair

68

Fig. 6–19 Fitting Leg to Chair Seat

Fig. 6–20 Installing Upright to Back

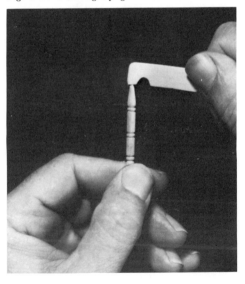

DEACON'S BENCH OR SETTEE

The deacon's bench is a functional piece of furniture for either the living room or dining room. The one shown in Fig.

6–21 is of the same basic construction as the rocking chair.

MATERIALS

PART		DIMENSIONS	QUANTITY
A	Back	$\frac{3}{32} \times \frac{3}{8} \times 4$	1
B	Seat	$\frac{3}{16} \times 1\frac{1}{2} \times 3\frac{1}{2}$	1
C	Upright	$\frac{5}{32}$ dia. dowel × $1\frac{9}{16}$	2
D	Spokes	$\frac{3}{32}$ dia. dowel × $1\frac{1}{2}$	7
E	Leg	$\frac{5}{32}$ dia. dowel × $1\frac{3}{8}$	4
F	Brace	$\frac{1}{8}$ dia. dowel × $1\frac{5}{16}$	2
G	Stretcher	$\frac{3}{32}$ dia. dowel × $3\frac{5}{16}$	1
H	Arm Support	$\frac{1}{8}$ dia. dowel × $\frac{5}{8}$	2
I	Arm Support	$\frac{1}{8}$ dia. dowel × $\frac{9}{16}$	2
J	Arm	$\frac{1}{8} \times \frac{3}{16} \times 1\frac{5}{8}$	2

CONSTRUCTION

1. Cut back **A** to length. Then cut shape (Fig. 6–23) with jigsaw or knife. Drill hole pattern as indicated.
2. Cut seat **B** to dimensions. Then drill hole pattern on top side, $\frac{1}{16}$ inch deep (Fig. 6–24). Next, drill hole pattern on bottom side $\frac{1}{16}$ inch deep (Fig. 6–25) then round corners.
3. Cut two uprights **C** to length. Then shape (Fig. 6–22) with knife and sandpaper. Taper top end to $\frac{3}{64}$ inch diameter and bottom end to $\frac{1}{16}$ inch diameter.
4. Cut seven spokes **D** to length and taper ends (Fig. 6–22) to $\frac{3}{64}$ inch diameter with sandpaper.
5. Cut four legs **E** to length and shape (Fig.

69

Fig. 6–21 Deacon's Bench or Settee

6–22) with knife. Drill one hole $\frac{3}{64}$ inch diameter in each leg, at location shown.

6. Cut two braces **F** to length. Then shape with knife (Fig. 6–22). Drill one $\frac{3}{64}$ inch diameter hole in center. Taper ends to $\frac{3}{64}$ inch diameter.

7. Cut stretcher **G** to length and taper ends to $\frac{3}{64}$ inch diameter.

8. Cut two arm supports **H** and **I** to length. Then shape with a knife to pattern (Fig. 6–22).

9. Cut arm **J** to pattern (Fig. 6–22). Round

top edges and notch end to match upright **C**.

10. Sand parts and stain to desired color.

ASSEMBLY

1. Attach one brace **F** between two legs **E** (Fig. 6–26) with glue. Make two assemblies.

2. Glue assembled legs to bottom of seat **B**.

3. With legs in position, establish length

70

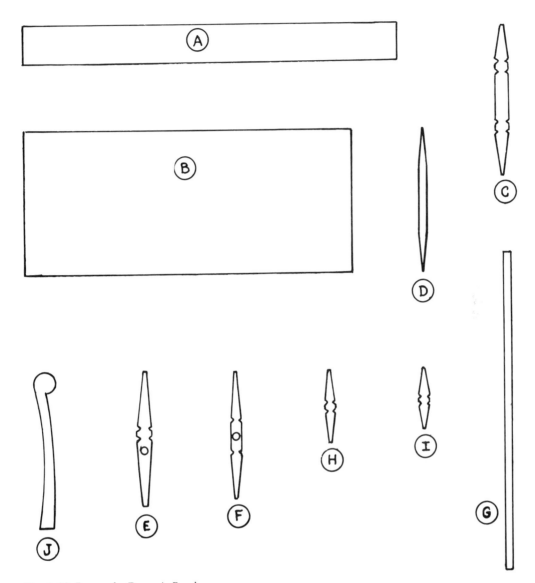

Fig. 6–22 Pattern for Deacon's Bench

of stretcher **G**. Then cut to length and attach to brace **F** with glue.

4. Glue uprights and spokes **C** and **D** to back **A**. Then insert entire assembly into bench seat.

5. Insert arm supports **H** and **I** into seat

to locate the hole pattern in arm **J**. Drill two $\frac{3}{64}$ inch diameter holes in each arm, and shape end to fit upright. Glue arm to assembly (Fig. 6–27).

6. Apply a light coat of satin finish with spray can. Buff with steel wool.

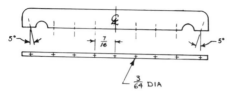

Fig. 6–23 Detail of Deacon's Bench Back

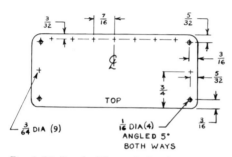

Fig. 6–24 Detail of Deacon's Bench Seat Top

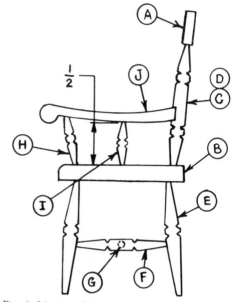

Fig. 6–26 Assembling Deacon's Bench

Fig. 6–27 Installing Arm on Deacon's Bench

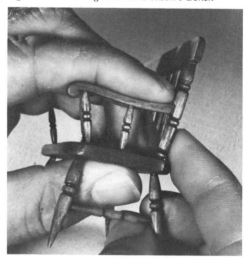

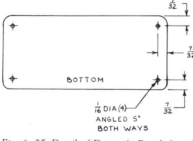

Fig. 6–25 Detail of Deacon's Bench Seat Bottom

DESK

The desk (Fig. 6–28) is a sturdily built piece of furniture, with the legs and the top measuring $2\frac{1}{4}$ inches in scale. Its massive appearance allows it to be displayed in either the den or the living room.

MATERIALS

PART		DIMENSIONS	QUANTITY
A	Leg	$\frac{3}{16} \times 1\frac{1}{2} \times 2\frac{1}{4}$	2
B	Top	$\frac{3}{16} \times 1\frac{3}{4} \times 4$	1
C	Shelf	$\frac{3}{16} \times \frac{3}{4} \times 3\frac{1}{4}$	1
D	Support	$\frac{1}{8} \times 1\frac{1}{2} \times 3\frac{1}{4}$	1
E	Back	$\frac{3}{16} \times \frac{5}{8} \times 4$	1
F	End	$\frac{3}{16} \times 1 \times 1\frac{9}{16}$	2
G	Base	$\frac{3}{16} \times \frac{3}{8} \times 1\frac{9}{16}$	2
H	Drawer Front	$\frac{1}{8} \times \frac{5}{8} \times 3\frac{5}{8}$	1
I	Drawer Side	$\frac{1}{16} \times \frac{13}{32} \times 1\frac{1}{2}$	2
J	Drawer Back	$\frac{1}{16} \times \frac{13}{32} \times 3\frac{1}{16}$	1
K	Drawer Bottom	$\frac{1}{16} \times 1\frac{1}{4} \times 3\frac{1}{16}$	1

Fig. 6–28 Desk

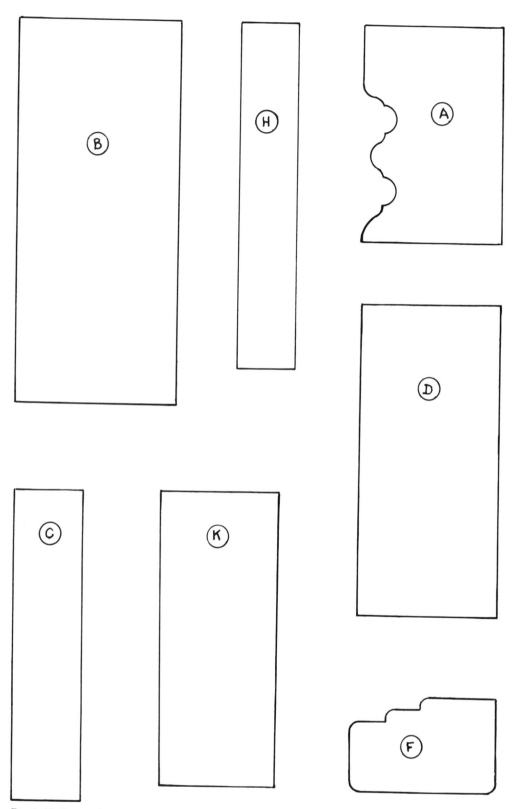

Fig. 6–29 Pattern for Desk

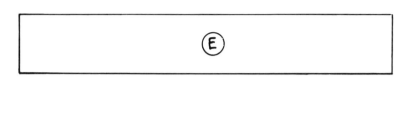

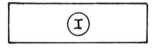

G

Fig. 6–29 continued

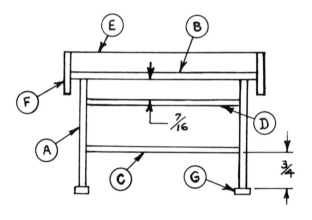

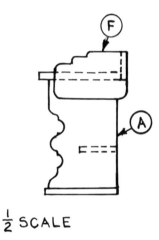

½ SCALE

Fig. 6–30 Assembling Desk

CONSTRUCTION

1. Cut legs **A** to pattern (Fig. 6–29) with jigsaw. Sand inside edges with sandpaper wrapped around a dowel to maintain identical pattern.

2. Cut ends **F** to pattern (Fig. 6–29) with jigsaw. Use three-cornered file on inside corners.

3. Cut remaining pieces to dimensions indicated.

4. Sand parts and stain to desired color.

ASSEMBLY

1. Glue shelf and support **C** and **D** flush to back edges of legs **A** and position to dimensions (Fig. 6–30).

75

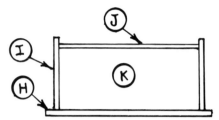

Fig. 6–31 Desk Drawer Assembly

2. Glue top **B** flush to back side of legs **A** and centered.

3. Glue back **E** against top and flush with legs.

4. Glue ends **F** to top **B** and flush with back **E**.

5. Glue bases **G** to bottom of each leg **A**.

6. Assemble drawer parts **H**, **I**, **J**, and **K** (Fig. 6–31) with sides **I** flush with top of drawer front **H** and centered.

7. Assemble drawer in place and apply a finish coat.

8. Place drawer pull on drawer front.

C	Rung	$\frac{1}{8}$ dia. dowel × $1\frac{7}{16}$	2
D	Brace	$\frac{3}{32}$ dia. dowel × $1\frac{5}{16}$	1
E	Spoke	$\frac{3}{32}$ dia. dowel × $\frac{7}{8}$	6
F	Support	$\frac{1}{8}$ dia. dowel × $\frac{15}{16}$	2
G	Arm	$\frac{1}{8}$ × 2 × 2	1
H	Back	$\frac{1}{4}$ × 1 × 2	1

CAPTAIN'S CHAIR

The captain's chair (Fig. 6–32) is an ideal accessory for the den, living room or dining room. It can be utilized as an accent chair in the living room or as a desk chair in the den. It will also mix nicely in the dining room with a variety of table styles. This chair, finished in fruitwood, is shown in the color section.

MATERIALS

PART		DIMENSIONS	QUANTITY
A	Seat	$\frac{3}{16}$ × $1\frac{5}{8}$ × $1\frac{5}{8}$	1
B	Leg	$\frac{5}{32}$ dia. dowel × $1\frac{7}{16}$	4

Fig. 6–32 Captain's Chair

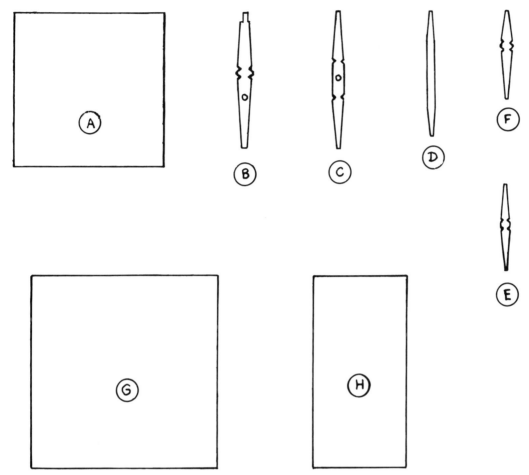

Fig. 6–33 *Pattern for Captain's Chair*

CONSTRUCTION

1. Cut seat **A** to dimension specified. If contoured seat is desired, see Chapter 4 before cutting outline of seat. Drill hole pattern on bottom of seat **A** (Fig. 6–34). Then drill hole pattern on the top side of seat (Fig. 6–35). *Then* cut outline of chair seat.

2. Cut four legs **B** to length, and shape (Fig. 6–33). Drill one $\frac{1}{16}$ inch diameter hole in each leg at location shown.

3. Cut two rungs **C** to length, and shape (Fig. 6–33). Drill one $\frac{3}{64}$ inch diameter hole in center of each rung.

4. Cut one brace **D** to length and taper ends with sandpaper to $\frac{3}{64}$ inch diameter (Fig. 6–33).

5. Cut six spokes **E** to length. Then shape. (Fig. 6–33). Taper ends to $\frac{3}{64}$ inch diameter.

6. Cut arm **G** to square blank. Then *draw* outline of arm shape on blank (Fig.

77

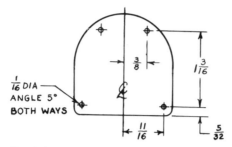

Fig. 6–34 Captain's Chair Seat Hole Pattern, Bottom

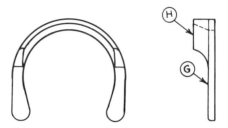

Fig. 6–37 Arm and Back Assembly for Captain's Chair

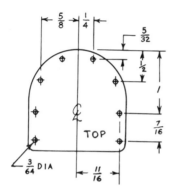

Fig. 6–35 Captain's Chair Seat Hole Pattern, Top

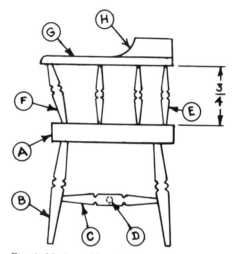

Fig. 6–38 Assembling Captain's Chair

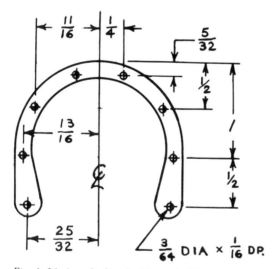

Fig. 6–36 Arm Outline for Captain's Chair

6–36). Determine drill hole pattern. *Then* cut outline with jigsaw.

7. Glue back (blank) **H** on top of arm outline, and then match outline with jigsaw. Shape assembly with a knife and sandpaper to pattern (Fig. 6–37). Sand assembly smooth.

8. Cut two supports **F** to length, and shape (Fig. 6–33). Taper ends to $\frac{3}{64}$ inch diameter.

9. Stain parts to desired color. Fruitwood recommended.

ASSEMBLY

1. Glue brace **D** to Rungs **C** (Fig. 6–38). Glue rungs to legs **B**. Glue leg assemblies into chair seat **A**.
2. Glue spokes **E** and supports **F** into arm assembly **G** and **H** in position indicated. Insert and glue this assembly to chair seat **A** while holding arm parallel with seat (Fig. 6–38).
3. Apply a light coat of satin finish spray varnish; when dry, buff with steel wool.

WOODCARVER'S CHAIR

The dimensions for the woodcarver's chair (Fig. 6–39) were obtained by visiting an antique store. It has a trapezoidal shaped seat, which requires the special caning pattern described in Chapter 4.

MATERIALS

PART		DIMENSIONS	QUANTITY
A	Back Leg	$\frac{5}{16}$ dia. dowel $\times 3\frac{5}{8}$	2
B	Front Leg	$\frac{5}{16}$ dia. dowel $\times 1\frac{15}{16}$	2
C	Back, Top	$\frac{3}{32} \times \frac{9}{16} \times 1\frac{3}{8}$	1
D	Back, Bottom	$\frac{3}{32} \times \frac{5}{16} \times 1\frac{3}{8}$	1
E	Spokes	$\frac{3}{32}$ dia. dowel $\times 1$	4
F	Back Rung	$\frac{3}{32}$ dia. dowel $\times 1\frac{3}{8}$	2
G	Side Rung	$\frac{3}{32}$ dia. dowel $\times 1\frac{9}{16}$	2
H	Stretcher	$\frac{1}{8}$ dia. dowel $\times 1\frac{9}{16}$	2
I	Front Rung	$\frac{3}{32}$ dia. dowel $\times 1\frac{3}{4}$	1
J	Front Brace	$\frac{1}{16} \times \frac{3}{8} \times 1\frac{3}{4}$	1
K	Arms	$\frac{1}{8} \times \frac{5}{16} \times 2$	2

Fig. 6–39 Woodcarver's Chair

CONSTRUCTION

1. Cut two back legs **A** to length. Then drill hole pattern (Fig. 6–42). Remove the $\frac{1}{8}$ inch web between the two sets of holes on each leg with a knife. Then shape leg (Fig. 6–40).
2. Cut two front legs **B** to length. Then drill hole pattern (Fig. 6–43). Remove the $\frac{1}{8}$ inch web between the two holes on each leg with a knife. Then shape leg (Fig. 6–40).
3. Cut back top **C** to pattern (Fig. 6–40) with a jigsaw. Drill hole pattern (Fig. 6–41) and notch ends to dimensions indicated.
4. Cut back bottom **D** to pattern (Fig.

79

6–40) with a jigsaw. Drill hole pattern (Fig. 6–41) and notch ends to dimensions indicated.

5. Cut four spokes **E** to pattern with a knife (Fig. 6–40). Taper ends to $\frac{3}{64}$ inch diameter.

6. Cut back rungs **F** to length. Then shape both ends of each rung with a knife (Fig. 6–44).

7. Cut side rungs **G** to length. Then shape both ends of each rung with a knife (Fig. 6–44).

8. Cut stretcher **H** to length. Then shape with a knife, and taper ends to $\frac{1}{16}$ inch diameter with sandpaper.

9. Cut front rung **I** to length. Then shape both ends with a knife to pattern (Fig. 6–44).

10. Cut front brace **J** to pattern (Fig. 6–40) with a jigsaw.

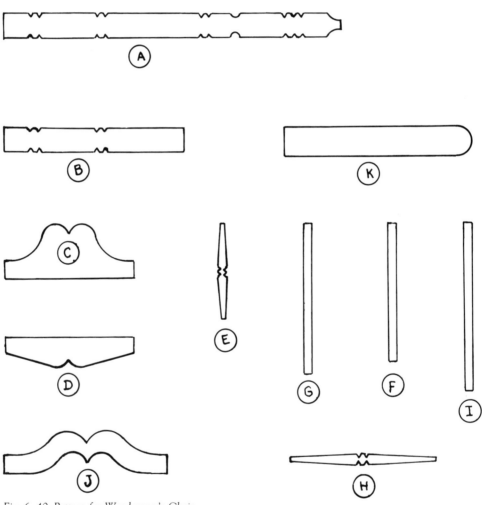

Fig. 6–40 *Pattern for Woodcarver's Chair*

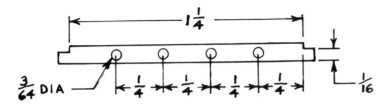

SCALE: 2×SIZE

Fig. 6–41 *Detail of Back Hole Pattern*

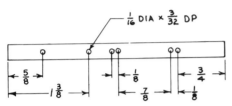

Fig. 6–42 *Back Leg Hole Pattern*

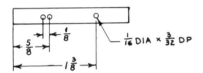

Fig. 6–43 *Front Leg Hole Pattern*

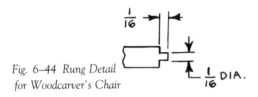

Fig. 6–44 *Rung Detail for Woodcarver's Chair*

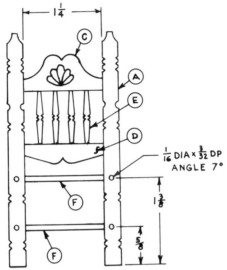

Fig. 6–46 *Assembling Back Legs of Woodcarver's Chair*

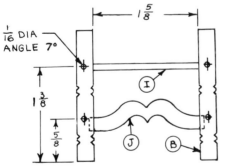

Fig. 6–45 *Assembling Front Legs of Woodcarver's Chair*

11. Cut arms **K** to pattern shown, and add a cut on the square end to match back leg (see picture of chair).

12. Stain parts to desired color or leave natural.

ASSEMBLY

1. Attach front rung and brace **I** and **J** between front legs **B** with glue (Fig. 6–45).

2. Attach spokes **E** with glue between top and bottom parts of back **C** and **D**. Glue this assembly into back legs **A** while

81

inserting rungs **F** (Fig. 6–46). Square and clamp assembly to dry. Woodburn or carve design on top back as shown.

3. Drill holes in both back legs, angled 7° outward (Fig. 6–46).

4. Drill holes in both front legs, angled 7° inward (Fig. 6–45).

5. Glue rungs **G** in the top holes and stretchers **H** in the lower holes between the front and back legs to complete the chair assembly.

6. Apply a light coat of spray varnish.

7. See Chapter 4 for details on caning chair seats.

SPINNING WHEEL

The spinning wheel (Fig. 6–47) is the most challenging project in this book.

MATERIALS

PART		DIMENSIONS	QUANTITY
A	Table	$\frac{1}{4} \times \frac{3}{4} \times 1\frac{5}{8}$	1
B	Upright	$\frac{5}{32}$ dia. dowel $\times 1\frac{7}{8}$	2
C	Leg	$\frac{5}{32}$ dia. dowel $\times 1\frac{5}{8}$	3
D	Bearing Housing	$\frac{5}{32}$ dia. dowel $\times \frac{7}{8}$	2
E	Support	$\frac{5}{32}$ dia. dowel $\times 1\frac{3}{32}$	1
F	Pulley	$\frac{3}{16}$ dia. dowel $\times \frac{5}{8}$	1
G	Bobbin	$\frac{3}{32} \times \frac{1}{2} \times \frac{9}{16}$	1
H	Base	$\frac{3}{8}$ dia. dowel $\times \frac{7}{16}$	1
I	Bearing	$\frac{3}{64} \times \frac{7}{32} \times \frac{9}{16}$ (leather)	2
J	Peg	$\frac{1}{16}$ dia. dowel $\times \frac{7}{16}$	1
K	Flywheel	2 dia. $\times \frac{7}{32}$ thick	1
L	Hub	$\frac{7}{16}$ dia. $\times \frac{5}{16}$ thick	1
M	Spoke	$\frac{3}{32}$ dia. dowel $\times \frac{5}{8}$	8
N	Treadle	$\frac{1}{32} \times \frac{3}{16} \times \frac{3}{4}$	1
O	Brace	$\frac{1}{16} \times \frac{1}{8} \times 1\frac{5}{8}$	1
P	Pivot	$\frac{5}{32} \times \frac{5}{32} \times 1\frac{11}{16}$	1
Q	Pitman	$\frac{1}{16} \times \frac{5}{32} \times 2\frac{3}{8}$	1
R	Handle	$\frac{1}{8}$ dia. dowel $\times \frac{1}{2}$	1
S	Pin	$1\frac{1}{2}$ inch craft pin (purchased)	2

CONSTRUCTION

1. Cut table **A** to size, and drill through holes on top side (Fig. 6–49). Drill holes on bottom (Fig. 6–50).

2. Cut two uprights **B** to length. Then shape to pattern (Fig. 6–48) with a knife. Shape ends to $\frac{3}{32}$ inch diameter to fit holes in table **A**.

3. Cut three legs **C** to length. Then shape to pattern (Fig. 6–48) with a knife. Shape small ends to $\frac{3}{32}$ inch diameter to fit holes in table.

4. Cut bearing housing **D** to pattern (Fig. 6–51) with a knife. Drill holes through, and remove web between holes with a knife to form a slot.

5. Cut support **E** to pattern (Fig. 6–52) with a knife. Then drill holes as located.

6. Cut pulley **F** to pattern (Fig. 6–48) with a knife. Then drill a hole through the center with a #72 drill.

7. Cut bobbin **G** to pattern (Fig. 6–48) with a knife or jigsaw. Drill hole through base of "U" using a #72 drill.

8. Cut base **H**. Then shape (Fig. 6–53) to mate with support **E**.

9. Cut bearing **I** from leather to pattern (Fig. 6–48). Drill hole using #72 drill.

10. Cut peg **J** to length and round one end.

11. Cut flywheel **K** on a lathe or jigsaw. Shape with a knife to pattern (Fig.

Fig. 6–47 Spinning Wheel

6–54) if a jigsaw is used. Use an awl to locate hole position. With a pin vise, drill holes from the inside $\frac{3}{32}$ inch deep.

12. Cut hub **L** to pattern (Fig. 6–55) with a knife or lathe. Drill required holes $\frac{3}{32}$ inch deep.

13. Cut spokes **M** to pattern (Fig. 6–48) and shape with a knife.

14. Cut treadle **N** to pattern (Fig. 6–48) with a jigsaw or a knife.

15. Cut brace **O** to length. (Required angle cut will be done at assembly.)

16. Cut pivot **P** to length. Then shape (Fig. 6–57). Cut angle groove deep enough to accept brace **O**.

17. Cut pitman **Q** to pattern (Fig. 6–56), with jigsaw or a knife. Drill required holes as shown.

18. Cut handle **R** to pattern (Fig. 6–48) with a knife.

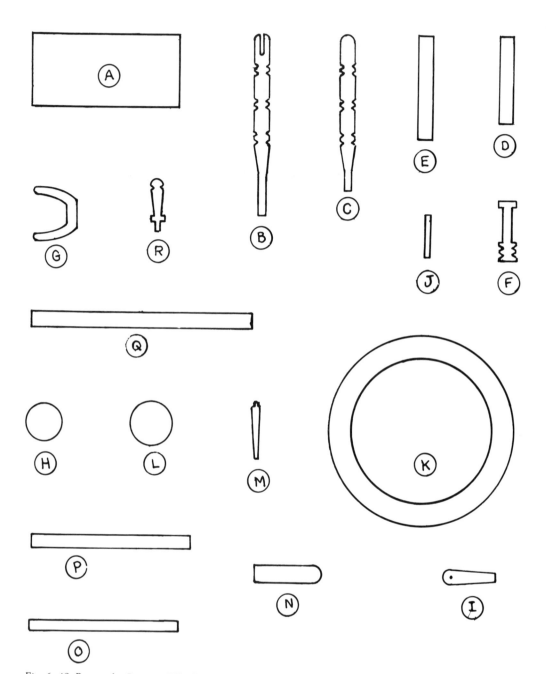

Fig. 6–48 Pattern for Spinning Wheel

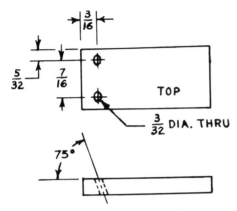

Fig. 6–49 Top Hole Pattern for Table

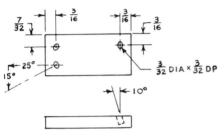

Fig. 6–50 Bottom Hole Pattern for Table

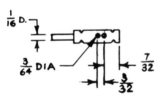

Fig. 6–51 Detail of Bearing Housing

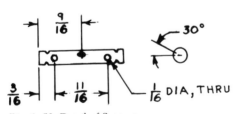

Fig. 6–52 Detail of Support

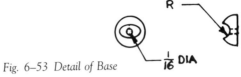

Fig. 6–53 Detail of Base

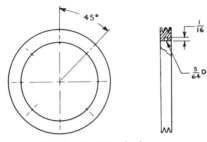

Fig. 6–54 Detail of Flywheel

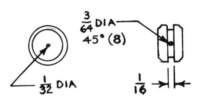

Fig. 6–55 Detail of Hub

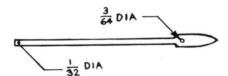

Fig. 6–56 Detail of Pitman

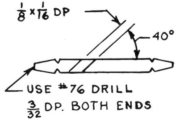

Fig. 6–57 Detail of Pivot

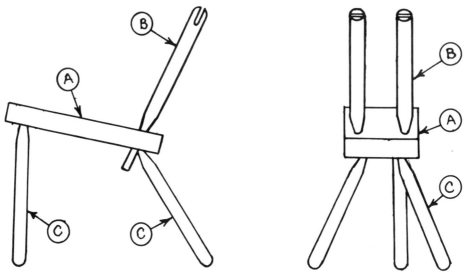

Fig. 6–58 Assembling Table, Uprights, and Legs of Spinning Wheel

19. Sandpaper parts, and stain desired color.

Fig. 6–60 Spinning Wheel Bobbin Alignment

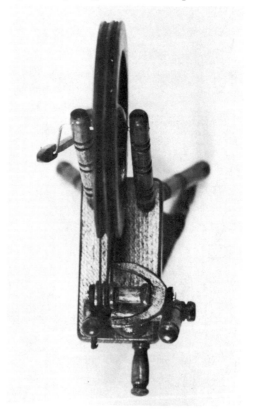

ASSEMBLY

1. Glue uprights **B** into top of table **A** (Fig. 6–58). Place legs **C** in bottom of table as shown.

2. The flywheel is assembled with a snug fit. Lightly assemble spokes **M** to hub **L** with small amount of glue (Fig. 6–59) and align with holes in the flywheel **K**. As pressure is applied to the hub, keep spokes aligned. Adjust length of spokes if necessary. Hub should align in center of flywheel.

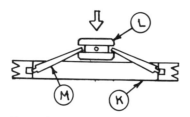

Fig. 6–59 Assembling Flywheel, Spokes, and Hub

86

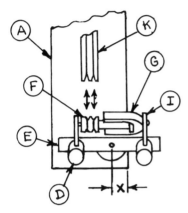

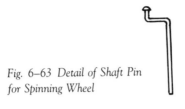

Fig. 6–63 *Detail of Shaft Pin for Spinning Wheel*

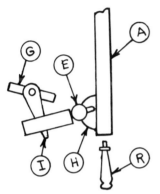

Fig. 6–61 *Spinning Wheel Bobbin Assembly*

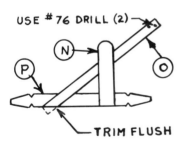

USE #76 DRILL (2)

TRIM FLUSH

Fig. 6–62 *Assembling Treadle Pivot*

3. To assemble bobbin, refer to Figs. 6–60 and 6–61. Insert the two bearing housings **D** with glue into holes of support **E**.

4. Then insert one bearing **I** with glue into each bearing housing **D**, and allow to protrude (Fig. 6–61).

5. Install bobbin **G** and Pulley **F** between bearings **I** with craft pin **S**. Trim pin to length.

6. Position this assembly on table **A** so that pulley will align with flywheel (indicated by arrows). Locate position of "X" in Fig. 6–61, and drill $\frac{1}{16}$ inch diameter hole in table to attach bobbin assembly with peg **J**. Insert peg thru support **E**, attach base **H**, and glue in place.

7. Drill hole in end of table and insert handle **R**.

8. Glue pivot, brace, and treadle **N, O** and **P** together (Fig. 6–62), and trim brace as indicated. Insert this assembly between rear and right leg, and establish location of holes to match pivot. Drill holes in legs and insert #24 gauge wire. Then trim wire to length.

9. Form Pin **S** (Fig. 6–63). Insert pin through hole in pitman **Q** and hub of flywheel assembly, and place in grooves of uprights. Attach pitman to brace with thread.

10. Wrap one strand of thread around pulley **F** and around flywheel assembly, and tie or glue ends.

11. Apply a light spray coat of varnish.

87

CHAPTER 7

Bedroom Group

The bedroom group consists of the pillar bed, nightstand, blanket chest, dresser, and trunk (Figs. 7–1, 7–2, and 7–3).

Each of the pieces selected for this group contains as many realistic details as possible. The massive pillars of the bed shows its ruggedness. The wood-burned relief pattern on the front of the blanket chest is a reminder of the past. The trunk's removable tray and leather handles add realism. The dresser's working drawers and pivoting mirror are characteristics desired by most miniaturists.

PILLAR BED

Before starting the pillar bed project, refer to Chapter 4 on spindle making. The bed is shown in Fig. 7–4, complete with comforter and pillows. The bed in Fig. 7–5 contains a mattress cut from $\frac{3}{8}$ inch foam plastic.

MATERIALS

PART		DIMENSIONS	QUANTITY
A	*Headboard*	$\frac{3}{32} \times 1\frac{3}{4} \times 4\frac{3}{8}$	1
B	*Footboard*	$\frac{3}{32} \times 1 \times 4\frac{3}{8}$	1
C	*Support*	$\frac{1}{16} \times 4 \times 6\frac{3}{16}$	1

Fig. 7–1 Bed Room Furniture Group: Pillar Bed, Nightstand, Blanket Chest, Rocking Chair, and Dresser

Fig. 7–2 Bed Room Furniture Group: Dresser, Nightstand, Rocking Chair, and Accessories

Fig. 7–3 Bed Room Furniture Group: Nightstand, Bed, and Dresser

D	Bracket Corner	$\frac{3}{32} \times \frac{3}{4} \times \frac{3}{4}$	4
E	Headboard Leg	$\frac{5}{16}$ dia. dowel $\times$ 5	2
F	Footboard Leg	$\frac{5}{16}$ dia. dowel $\times$ $3\frac{1}{2}$	2
G	Headboard Trim	$\frac{5}{16}$ dia. dowel $\times$ $3\frac{3}{8}$	1
H	Side Rail	$\frac{3}{32} \times \frac{1}{2} \times 6\frac{3}{16}$	2
I	Brace	$\frac{3}{32} \times \frac{5}{16} \times 6\frac{3}{16}$	2

CONSTRUCTION

1. Cut headboard **A** to dimensions listed and to pattern (Fig. 7–6). Sand with the grain of the wood.

2. Cut footboard **B** to dimensions listed and to pattern (Fig. 7–6). Sand with the grain of the wood.

3. Cut headboard leg **E** to length. Then shape with knife or wood lathe to pattern (Fig. 7–7). Refer to Chapter 4 on how to shape spindles. Drill $\frac{3}{32}$ inch diameter holes, $\frac{3}{32}$ inch deep, at locations indicated. Remove remaining web between holes with a knife, to appear as shown.

4. Cut footboard leg **F** to length. Then shape with knife or wood lathe to pattern (Fig. 7–8). Drill $\frac{3}{32}$ inch diameter holes, $\frac{3}{32}$ inch deep, at locations indicated. Remove remaining web between holes with a knife, to appear as shown.

5. Cut headboard trim **G** to length. Then shape with a knife or wood lathe to the pattern (Fig. 7–9). Drill $\frac{3}{32}$ inch diameter holes at locations indicated, and

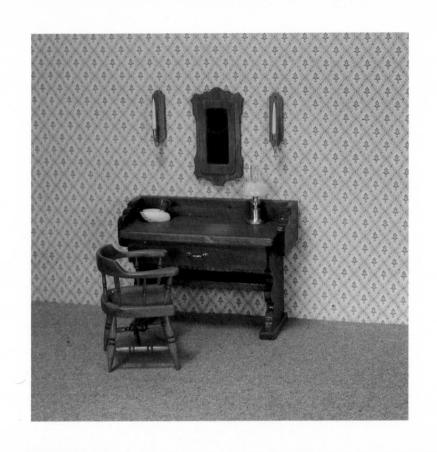

Fig. 7–4 Pillar Bed Assembly

remove remaining web between holes with a knife, to appear as shown.

6. To cut corner brackets **D**, cut two squares of $\frac{3}{4}$ inch, and then cut diagonally.

7. Cut remaining pieces to dimensions indicated.

8. Sand parts and stain to desired color.

ASSEMBLY

1. Glue headboard legs **E** to headboard **A**.

2. Glue headboard trim **G** to top of headboard **A**.

3. Glue footboard legs **F** to footboard **B**.

Fig. 7–5 Pillar Bed

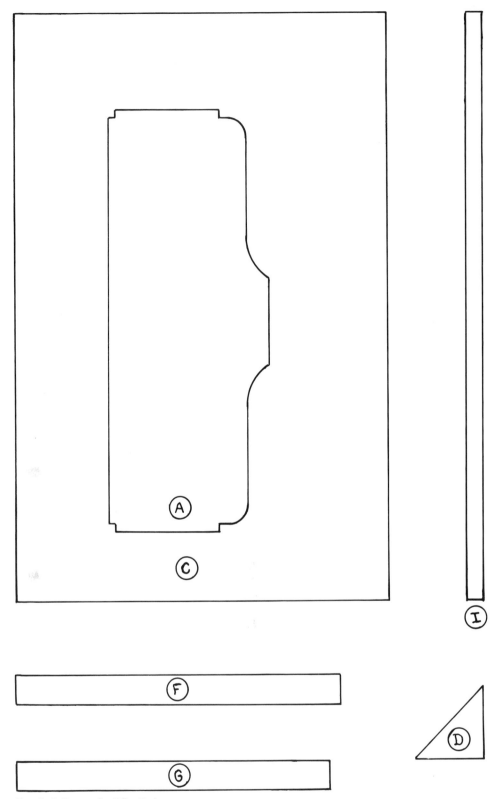

Fig. 7–6 Pattern for Pillar Bed

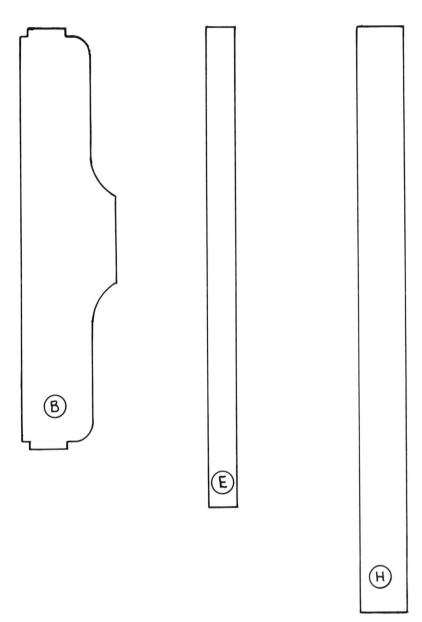

Fig. 7–6 continued

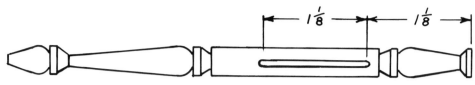

Fig. 7–7 Pattern for Headboard Leg

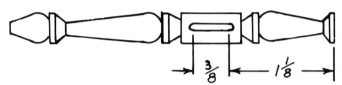

Fig. 7–8 Pattern for Footboard Leg

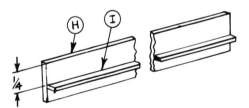

Fig. 7–9 Pattern for Headboard Trim

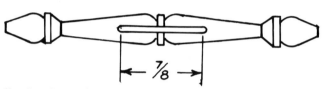

Fig. 7–10 Assembling Side Rail and Brace

4. Glue side rail **H** and brace **I** together (Fig. 7–10). Make two assemblies, and attach one to each side of support **C**.

5. Glue side rail and support assembly to headboard, with side rail flush at the bottom and centered between the legs. Glue footboard assembly to opposite end, centered between legs with side rail flush with bottom of footboard.

6. Glue corner brackets **D** to corners of support **C** on the bottom side.

7. When glue has dried, apply a light coat of satin finish spray varnish. Then buff lightly with steel wool.

A mattress may be provided for the pillar bed with a piece of foam rubber or plastic measuring 4 inches by 6 inches.

NIGHTSTAND

The night stand (Fig. 7–11), with its working drawer, is relatively easy to make.

MATERIALS

PART		DIMENSIONS	QUANTITY
A	Leg	$\frac{1}{8} \times 1\frac{1}{4} \times 1\frac{7}{8}$	2
B	Top	$\frac{1}{8} \times 1\frac{3}{8} \times 1\frac{3}{4}$	1
C	Shelf	$\frac{3}{32} \times 1\frac{1}{4} \times 1\frac{1}{4}$	1
D	Strut	$\frac{3}{32} \times 1\frac{1}{8} \times 1\frac{1}{4}$	1
E	Drawer Front	$\frac{3}{32} \times \frac{1}{2} \times 1\frac{3}{16}$	1
F	Drawer Side	$\frac{1}{32} \times \frac{1}{4} \times 1$	2
G	Drawer Back	$\frac{1}{32} \times \frac{1}{4} \times 1\frac{1}{8}$	1
H	Drawer Bottom	$\frac{1}{16} \times 1 \times 1\frac{3}{16}$	1

CONSTRUCTION

1. Cut legs **A** to pattern (Fig. 7–12).
2. Cut top **B** to dimension. Then round top edges.
3. Cut remaining parts to dimensions indicated.
4. Sand parts, and stain to desired color.

ASSEMBLY

1. Glue legs, top, and shelf **A**, **B**, and **C** together to dimension (Fig. 7–13).
2. Glue strut **D** to dimension (Fig. 7–13).
3. Assemble drawer parts **E**, **F**, **G**, and **H** together (Fig. 7–14), with sides flush to top of drawer front.
4. Attach a miniature nail for drawer pull, and paint nail flat black.
5. Apply a light coat of spray varnish, and buff with steel wool.

Fig. 7–11 Night Stand

BLANKET CHEST

The blanket chest (Fig. 7–15) is a fine accessory for bedroom, den, or attic. This chest is relatively easy to make.

MATERIALS

PART		DIMENSIONS	QUANTITY
A	Top	$\frac{1}{8} \times 1\frac{1}{2} \times 3\frac{3}{16}$	1
B	Side	$\frac{1}{8} \times 1\frac{3}{16} \times 3$	2
C	Bottom	$\frac{1}{8} \times 1\frac{1}{2} \times 3\frac{3}{16}$	1
D	Base	$\frac{1}{8} \times \frac{7}{16} \times 3$	2
E	End	$\frac{1}{8} \times 1\frac{3}{16} \times 1\frac{5}{32}$	2
F	Leg	$\frac{1}{8} \times \frac{7}{16} \times 1\frac{5}{32}$	2
G	Hinge	(purchased)	2

CONSTRUCTION

1. Cut two bases **D** to pattern (Fig. 7–16).
2. Cut two legs **F** to pattern (Fig. 7–16).
3. Cut two sides **B**. Then select one and apply detail (Fig. 7–17) with waterproof

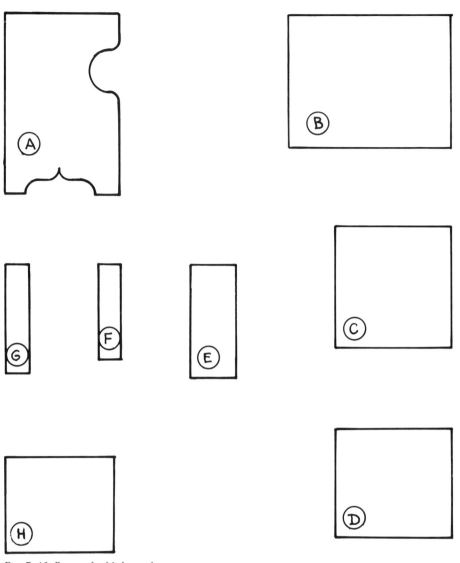

Fig. 7–12 Pattern for Nightstand

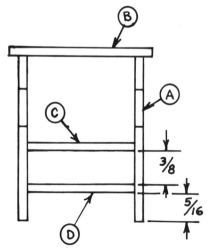

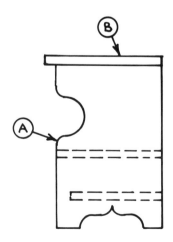

Fig. 7–13 Assembling Nightstand

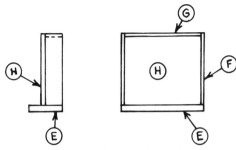

Fig. 7–14 Nightstand Drawer Assembly

ink, or woodburn pattern into side with a woodburning pen.

4. Cut remaining parts to dimensions indicated.

5. Sand parts, and stain to desired color.

ASSEMBLY

1. Glue sides and ends **B** and **E**, centered and flush to the back edge of bottom **C** (Fig. 7–17).

2. Glue bases and legs **D** and **F** flush to back of bottom **C**.

3. Locate hinges **G** on inside of top **A**. Then notch side **B**, as required for hinge clearance. Attach hinge with shortened

Fig. 7–15 Blanket Chest

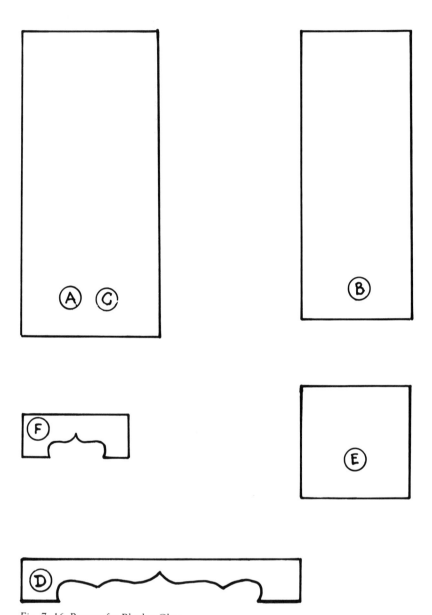

Fig. 7–16 Pattern for Blanket Chest

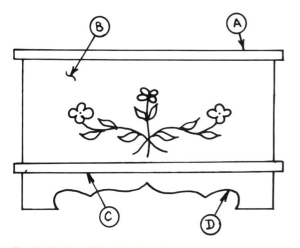 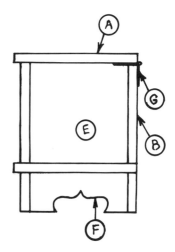

Fig. 7–17 Assembling Blanket Chest

nails or craft pins (Fig. 7–17). Fig. 7–18 shows hinges being installed.

4. Apply a light coat of spray varnish, and buff with steel wool. Apply a second coat of varnish if desired.

Fig. 7–18 Installing Hinges on Blanket Chest

DRESSER

The dresser, circa 1914, (Fig. 7–19) is included because of its attractiveness and simplicity. The exact date of its manufacture has not been established; the date given is based on the original, which still has a shipping label that indicates it was shipped from Chicago to South Dakota by rail in 1914.

MATERIALS

PART		DIMENSIONS	QUANTITY
A	Top and Bottom Guide	$\frac{1}{8} \times 1\frac{5}{8} \times 3\frac{3}{16}$	2
B	Drawer Support	$\frac{3}{32} \times 1\frac{7}{16} \times 3\frac{3}{16}$	2
C	Leg	$\frac{3}{16} \times \frac{3}{16} \times 2\frac{7}{8}$	4
D	Back	$\frac{1}{16} \times 1\frac{15}{16} \times 3\frac{3}{16}$	1
E	Top Spacer	$\frac{1}{16} \times \frac{1}{2} \times 1\frac{7}{16}$	2
F	Top Center Spacer	$\frac{1}{8} \times \frac{1}{2} \times 1\frac{7}{16}$	1
G	Lower Spacer	$\frac{1}{16} \times \frac{5}{8} \times 1\frac{7}{16}$	4

O	Front Lge. Drawer	$\frac{3}{32} \times \frac{5}{8} \times 3\frac{1}{8}$	1
P	Front Lge. Drawer	$\frac{3}{32} \times \frac{21}{32} \times 3\frac{1}{8}$	1
Q	Bottom Drawer	$\frac{1}{16} \times 1\frac{3}{16} \times 3$	2
R	Side Drawer	$\frac{1}{16} \times \frac{17}{32} \times 1\frac{3}{16}$	4
S	Back Drawer	$\frac{1}{16} \times \frac{17}{32} \times 2\frac{7}{8}$	2
T	Mirror Holder	$\frac{1}{8} \times 1\frac{13}{16} \times 2\frac{5}{8}$	1
U	Mirror Frame	$\frac{1}{32} \times 1\frac{13}{16} \times 2\frac{5}{8}$	1
V	Mirror Support	$\frac{1}{8} \times 1 \times 2\frac{1}{2}$	2
W	Stretcher	$\frac{1}{8} \times \frac{1}{2} \times 1\frac{7}{8}$	1
X	Back Support	$\frac{1}{32} \times \frac{3}{16} \times 1\frac{1}{4}$	2
Y	Brace	$\frac{1}{32} \times \frac{3}{16} \times 2\frac{7}{8}$	1
Z	Mirror	$\frac{3}{32} \times 1\frac{1}{2} \times 2$	1

Fig. 7–19 Dresser

H	Side Panel	$\frac{1}{8} \times 1\frac{1}{4} \times 2\frac{3}{16}$	2
I	Trim	$\frac{1}{32} \times \frac{3}{16} \times 1\frac{1}{4}$	4
J	Top	$\frac{3}{32} \times 1\frac{7}{8} \times 4$	1
K	Front Sm. Drawer	$\frac{3}{32} \times \frac{1}{2} \times 1\frac{1}{2}$	2
L	Bottom Sm. Drawer	$\frac{1}{16} \times 1\frac{3}{16} \times 1\frac{3}{8}$	2
M	Side Sm. Drawer	$\frac{1}{16} \times \frac{3}{8} \times 1\frac{3}{16}$	4
N	Back Sm. Drawer	$\frac{1}{16} \times \frac{3}{8} \times 1\frac{1}{4}$	2

CONSTRUCTION

1. Cut top **J** to pattern (Fig. 7–20).
2. Cut mirror **Z** to size using a glass cutter.
3. Using the mirror as a template, cut out the inside only of mirror holder **T**. Make this a snug fit with mirror.
4. Cut inside only of mirror frame **U** (Fig. 7–20). Then sand inside cut surface smooth. Center mirror frame on mirror holder and glue the two together. When the glue has dried, cut to outline mirror holder T (Fig. 7–20) using a jigsaw. Use extra-fine sandpaper to sand assembly smooth.
5. Cut mirror supports **V** with a jigsaw (Fig. 7–20). Round edges with extra-fine sandpaper.
6. Cut stretcher **W** with a jigsaw. Then match ends squarely with the mirror

Fig. 7–20 Pattern for Dresser

Fig. 7–20 continued

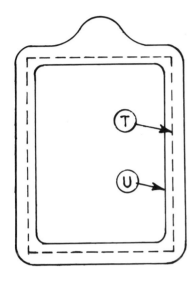

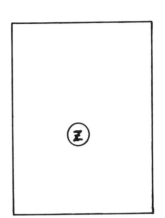

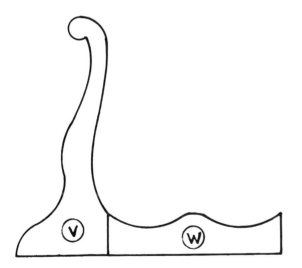

103

supports **V**. Round top edges with extra-fine sandpaper.

7. Cut remaining pieces to size. Sand and stain to desired color. Fruitwood oil stain recommended.

ASSEMBLY (BASE)

1. Build leg assemblies first (Fig. 7–21). Take two legs **C** and glue side panel **H** flush with top of leg. Place trim **I** flush with top and bottom of side panel. Clamp or apply weight to assembly until the glue has dried. Make two assemblies.

2. For ease in building the dresser base, assemble base in the *inverted* position. Start by placing top guide **A** on a flat surface. Then glue leg assemblies (in inverted position) in place.

3. Glue back **D** flush with inside of leg assemblies and top guide.

4. Glue top spacers **E** flush with back and against leg assembly. Locate spacer **F** in exact center of top guide.

5. Glue one drawer support **B** to leg assemblies and flush with back.

6. Glue two lower spacers **G**, one on each side, flush with back and against leg assemblies.

7. Glue remaining drawer support **B** flush with back and against leg assemblies.

8. Glue the two remaining lower spacers **G** flush with back and against leg assemblies.

9. Glue bottom guide **A** flush with back and with front and back of both leg assemblies. In inverted position, place a clamp or rubber band around the middle of the assembly and then add a weight until glue dries.

10. When the glue has dried, place top **J** (not shown on assembly) flush with back and centered with the leg assemblies and glue in place.

ASSEMBLY (DRAWERS)

1. Two small drawers are required. Assemble drawer parts **K**, **L**, **M**, and **N** (Fig. 7–22). Center parts on drawer front so that a $\frac{1}{16}$ inch space exists on each side and a $\frac{1}{32}$ inch space exists at top and bottom.

2. Glue bottom drawer parts **O**, **Q**, **R**, and **S** (Fig. 7–23), with equal spacing on each side. Assure drawer bottom is $\frac{1}{32}$ inch *below* drawer front. (This is done to equalize the vertical spacing of the drawer fronts.)

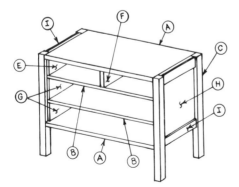

Fig. 7–21 Assembling Dresser Base

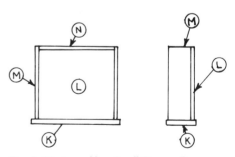

Fig. 7–22 Assembling Small Dresser Drawer

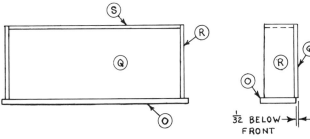

Fig. 7–23 Assembling Bottom Dresser Drawer

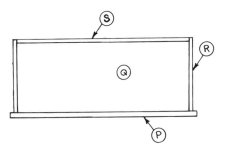

Fig. 7–24 Assembling Middle Dresser Drawer

3. Glue middle drawer parts **P**, **Q**, **R**, and **S** (Fig. 7–24), equally spaced on the sides as indicated.

ASSEMBLY (MIRROR)

1. Dry assemble parts together to assure proper fit before gluing. (Refer to Fig. 7–25.)
2. Align bottom edges of mirror supports **V** with stretcher **W**. Then glue together.
3. On the back side of the mirror assembly, center the brace **Y**, and glue in place. Place the two back supports **X** in position shown and allow to project $\frac{3}{4}$ inch below bottom surface of stretcher.
4. Place mirror holder assembly in proper position and drill one hole on each side (using #72 drill bit) from the inside of mirror holder into mirror support, approximately $\frac{1}{16}$ inch. (Refer to Fig.

7–25.) Place short piece of wire on each side for a hinge pin. Trim flush with inside of mirror frame.

5. Center mirror assembly on base of dresser. Glue in place by adding a small

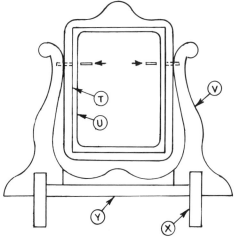

Fig. 7–25 Assembling Dresser Mirror Assembly

amount of glue to bottom of stretcher and back supports.

6. When glue has dried, apply a thin satin finish coat of spray varnish. Lightly buff with steel wool, and apply a second coat if desired.

7. Attach drawer pulls (purchase).

TRUNK

Most of the difficulty encountered in building a trunk is in making a lid that will match the dimensions of both the length and width of the bottom portion. This difficulty is removed by building the trunk as a box and then cutting in two. The two halves will match exactly, provided the box was square to begin with. The trunk is pictured in Fig. 7–26.

Fig. 7–26 Trunk

MATERIALS

PART		DIMENSIONS	QUANTITY
A	Bottom	$\frac{3}{32} \times 1\frac{1}{2} \times 2\frac{5}{16}$	1
B	Ends	$\frac{3}{32} \times 1\frac{1}{2} \times 1\frac{1}{2}$	2
C	Sides	$\frac{3}{32} \times 1\frac{1}{2} \times 2\frac{1}{2}$	2
D	Top	$\frac{3}{32} \times 1\frac{11}{16} \times 2\frac{1}{2}$	1
E	Rib End	$\frac{1}{32} \times \frac{3}{32} \times 1\frac{11}{16}$	4
F	Rib Side	$\frac{1}{32} \times \frac{3}{32} \times 2\frac{9}{16}$	4
G	Rib Top	$\frac{1}{32} \times \frac{5}{32} \times 1\frac{11}{16}$	2
H	Corner Brackets	foil $\frac{3}{32} \times \frac{3}{8}$	8
I	Handle (leather)	$\frac{1}{32} \times \frac{1}{8} \times 1$	2
J	Bracket	shim stock $\frac{3}{16} \times \frac{5}{16}$	2
K	Hinges	$\frac{5}{8}$ inch long (purchased)	2
L	Drawer Pulls	(purchased)	2
M	Drawer Pulls	(purchased)	2
N	Tray Stop	$\frac{1}{32} \times \frac{3}{32} \times 1$	2
O	Tray Bottom	$\frac{1}{32} \times 1\frac{3}{8} \times 2\frac{1}{4}$	1
P	Tray Side	$\frac{1}{32} \times \frac{3}{8} \times 2\frac{1}{4}$	2
Q	Tray End	$\frac{1}{32} \times \frac{11}{32} \times 1\frac{3}{8}$	2

CONSTRUCTION

1. Cut ribs **E**, **F**, and **G** in strips of proper width. Then sand smooth and stain a light oak color. When dry, cut to required lengths with razor blade.

2. Cut handle **I** from thin brown leather.

3. Cut handle brackets **J** to length from .002 inch shim stock or equivalent. Drill $\frac{1}{32}$ inch diameter hole in the center, and then form into a U shape to fit width of handle **I**.

4. Cut corner brackets **H** from paper-backed foil (cigarette pack is a good source) to pattern (Fig. 7–27). Aluminum foil can be used, but regular glue will not hold.

5. Cut remaining pieces to size (Fig. 7–27). Then sand smooth. Do not stain; leave natural.

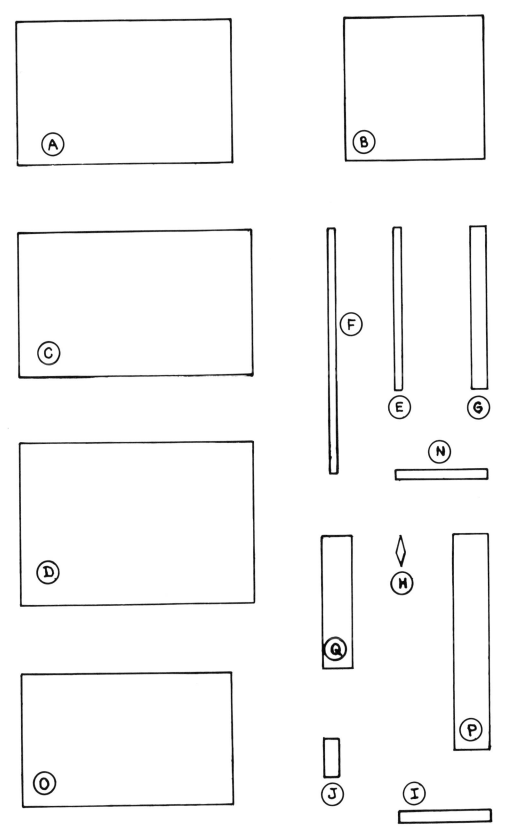

Fig. 7–27 Pattern for Trunk

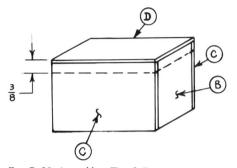

Fig. 7–28 Assembling Trunk Box

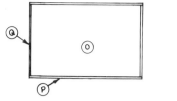

Fig. 7–30 Assembling Trunk Tray

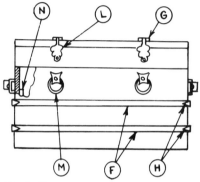

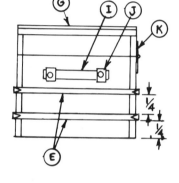

Fig. 7–29 Assembling Trunk

ASSEMBLY

1. For ease of assembly, construct the unit as a box. Then cut into two parts with table saw (Fig. 7–28).

2. Assemble bottom, ends, and sides **A**, **B**, and **C**. Make sure trunk is square. Then add top **D**. Allow glue to dry $\frac{1}{2}$ hour before cutting with saw.

3. Lightly sand saw cuts and paint exterior of the two parts with a flat black fast-drying paint. Set aside to dry overnight.

4. Glue ribs **E**, **F**, and **G** (Fig. 7–29).

5. Glue corner brackets **H** to corners, as shown.

6. Attach handle and bracket **I** and **J** with shortened nails or craft pins. Trim nails flush, or cleat, to inside.

7. Install hinges **K** and remaining hardware **L** and **M** as shown with shortened nails or craft pins.

8. Glue tray parts **O**, **P**, and **Q** (Fig. 7–30).

9. Apply wallpaper to the inside of the trunk, including lid and tray, with glue.

10. Glue tray stops **N** to inside of trunk, $\frac{5}{16}$ inch below the opening (Fig. 7–29).

11. Apply a light coat of satin finish spray varnish.

CHAPTER 8

Accessories

The accessories shown in Figs. 8–1 and 8–2 are described on the following pages. Most of these projects are fairly easy to make. The violin and guitar require a significant amount of carving with a knife.

SCONCE

A pair of sconces can enhance a wall or fireplace or complement a picture.

MATERIALS

PART		DIMENSIONS
A	*Back*	$\frac{3}{32} \times \frac{7}{16} \times 1\frac{7}{8}$
B	*Holder*	$\frac{3}{16}$ dia. dowel $\times \frac{9}{16}$
C	*Bar*	$\frac{3}{32}$ dia. dowel $\times \frac{5}{16}$
D	*Candle*	$\frac{3}{32}$ dia. dowel $\times 1$

CONSTRUCTION

1. Cut back **A** to outline (Fig. 8–3) with jigsaw. Drill two $\frac{3}{64}$ inch diameter holes at locations shown. (Tape together in pairs before cutting and sanding.)
2. For the holder **B** drill $\frac{3}{64}$ inch diameter holes, one in the top and one in the side, before shaping to pattern (Fig. 8–3).
3. Reduce both ends of the bar **C** to $\frac{3}{64}$ inch diameter (Fig. 8–3) with a knife.
4. Stain back, holder, and bar with a mahogany or maple stain.
5. Cut candle **D** to length, and then shape (Fig. 8–3). Paint with flat white paint.

ASSEMBLY

1. Glue bar **C** to holder and back **B** and **A**.
2. Glue candle **D** in place and add a short piece of black thread to simulate a burnt wick.
3. Apply a light coat of satin finish varnish.

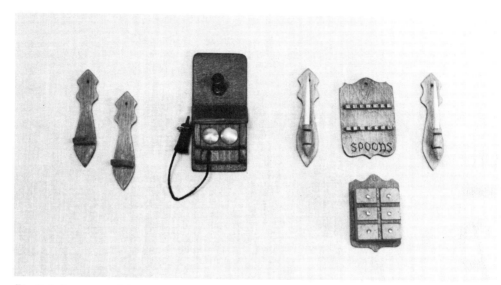

Fig. 8–1 Assortment of Accessories

Fig. 8–2 Assortment of Accessories

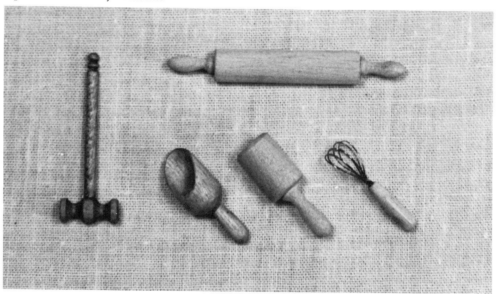

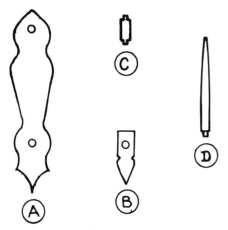

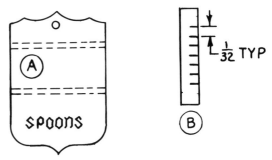

Fig. 8–4 Pattern for Spoon Holder

Fig. 8–3 Pattern for Sconce

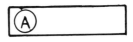

Fig. 8–5 Pattern for Rolling Pin

SPOON HOLDER

MATERIALS

PART	DIMENSIONS
A Back	$\frac{1}{16} \times 1 \times 1\frac{1}{2}$
B Holder (2)	$\frac{1}{32} \times \frac{7}{32} \times 1$

CONSTRUCTION

1. Cut back **A** to pattern (Fig. 8–4), and drill a $\frac{3}{64}$ inch diameter hole at the top.
2. Cut holder **B** to length. Then cut grooves as shown with a fine-toothed saw or knife. Cut several at one time to facilitate the cutting and to prevent breaking.
3. Sand smooth, and stain a mahogany or maple color.
4. Do the lettering on the back **A** with a fine-tipped pen and permanent ink.

ASSEMBLY

1. Glue the two holders **B** to the back **A** at locations indicated by the dotted lines.

2. Apply a light coat of satin finish varnish.

ROLLING PIN

MATERIALS

PART	DIMENSIONS
A Roller	$\frac{5}{16}$ dia. $\times 1\frac{1}{4}$
B Handle (2)	$\frac{1}{8}$ dia. $\times \frac{1}{2}$

CONSTRUCTION

1. Cut roller **A** to length (Fig. 8–5). Then drill $\frac{1}{16}$ inch diameter hole in each end.
2. Shape two handles **B** to pattern (Fig. 8–5).

ASSEMBLY

1. Apply glue to the end of each handle **B**, and insert one in each end of roller **A**.
2. Sand lightly and apply a light coat of spray varnish.

111

TELEPHONE

This telephone (Fig. 8–6) is from 1926.

MATERIALS

PART		DIMENSIONS	QUANTITY
A	Back	$\frac{1}{8} \times 1 \times 2\frac{3}{16}$	1
B	Side	$\frac{1}{8} \times \frac{3}{8} \times \frac{7}{8}$	2
C	Top	$\frac{1}{8} \times \frac{1}{2} \times 1$	1
D	Bell Housing	$\frac{1}{8} \times \frac{5}{8} \times \frac{3}{4}$	1
E	Front	$\frac{1}{8} \times \frac{5}{8} \times \frac{1}{2}$	1
F	Receiver	$\frac{1}{4}$ dia. dowel $\times \frac{1}{2}$	1
G	Mouthpiece	$\frac{1}{4}$ dia. dowel $\times \frac{5}{8}$	1
H	Rivets	$\frac{1}{4}$ dia. heads (purchased)	2

In addition, a small piece of #24 gauge wire and some black fishing line are required.

CONSTRUCTION

1. Cut back **A** to pattern (Fig. 8–7). Drill $\frac{1}{8}$ inch diameter hole centered as shown.
2. Cut two sides **B** to pattern (Fig. 8–8).

Fig. 8–6 Telephone

Drill a $\frac{3}{64}$ inch diameter hole in each piece at location shown.

3. Cut top **C** to dimensions specified.
4. Cut bell housing **D** to dimension. Then drill two $\frac{1}{8}$ inch diameter holes (Fig. 8–9).

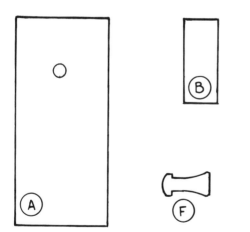
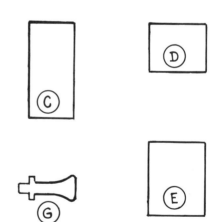

Fig. 8–7 Pattern for Telephone

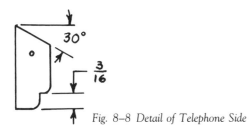

Fig. 8–8 Detail of Telephone Side

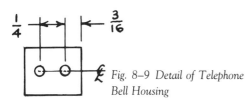

Fig. 8–9 Detail of Telephone
Bell Housing

Fig. 8–10 Detail of Receiver Holder

Fig. 8–11 Detail of Telephone Crank

5. Cut front **E** to dimensions specified.
6. Cut receiver **F** to length. Then shape (Fig. 8–7). Drill $\frac{1}{32}$ inch diameter hole in end for cord. Paint flat black.
7. Cut mouthpiece **G** to length. Then shape (Fig. 8–7). Paint flat black.
8. Shape wire for receiver holder (Fig. 8–10).
9. Shape wire for crank (Fig. 8–11).
10. Shorten shanks of rivets **H** if necessary.
11. Stain unpainted wood parts with a mahogany stain.

ASSEMBLY

1. Glue bell housing **D** and front **E** together and flush at the top. Then insert between the two sides **B**. Center this assembly on the back **A**, at the $\frac{1}{4}$ inch dimension (Fig. 8–12).

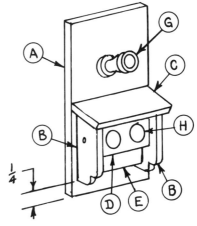

Fig. 8–12 Assembling Telephone

2. Bevel edge of top **C** to fit flush with the back **A**. Then glue in place.
3. Glue mouthpiece **G** in position shown.
4. Glue a $2\frac{1}{2}$ inch length of black fishing line to hole in receiver **F**, and attach other end to bottom of front **E**.
5. Install crank wire on right side **B**.
6. Install receiver wire on left side **B**.
7. Apply a light coat of satin finish varnish.

SPICE RACK

MATERIALS

PART		DIMENSIONS	QUANTITY
A	Back	$\frac{1}{16} \times 1 \times 1\frac{1}{2}$	1
B	Drawers	$\frac{1}{2} \times \frac{7}{8} \times \frac{15}{16}$	1
C	Craft Pins	$\frac{5}{8}$ inch long	6

CONSTRUCTION

1. Cut back **A** to pattern (Fig. 8–13). Drill $\frac{3}{64}$ inch diameter hole at the top.
2. Cut drawers **B** (Fig. 8–14), with table saw blade adjusted to $\frac{1}{16}$ inch height.
3. Sand and stain parts to desired color.

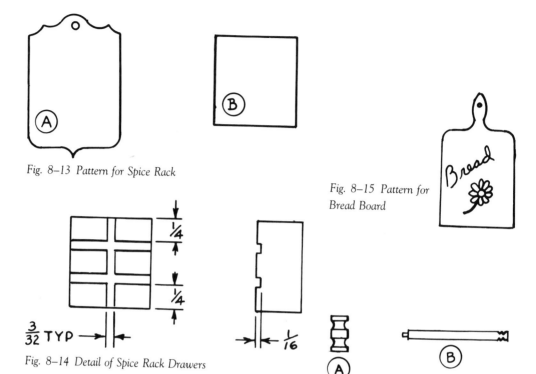

Fig. 8–13 Pattern for Spice Rack

Fig. 8–15 Pattern for Bread Board

Fig. 8–14 Detail of Spice Rack Drawers

Fig. 8–16 Pattern for Gavel

ASSEMBLY

1. Center drawers **B** on back **A**. Then glue in place.
2. Install shortened craft pins **C** as drawer pulls.
3. Apply a light coat of satin finish varnish.

BREAD BOARD

CONSTRUCTION

1. Cut bread board to pattern (Fig. 8–15). Drill $\frac{1}{32}$ inch diameter hole as shown.
2. Use fine-tipped pen to detail design with permanent ink.
3. Apply a light coat of satin finish varnish.

GAVEL

MATERIALS

PART		DIMENSIONS
A	Head	$\frac{3}{16}$ dia. $\times \frac{3}{8}$
B	Handle	$\frac{3}{32}$ dia. $\times 1\frac{3}{32}$

CONSTRUCTION

1. Cut head **A**, and shape (Fig. 8–16). Drill $\frac{3}{64}$ inch diameter hole in side.
2. Cut handle **B** (Fig. 8–16).
3. Sand, and stain desired color.

ASSEMBLY

1. Insert handle **B** with a drop of glue into the head **A**.
2. Apply a light coat of clear varnish.

114

Fig. 8–17 Pattern for Scoop

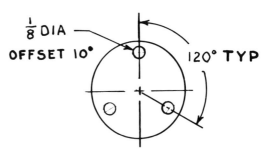

$\frac{1}{8}$ DIA — OFFSET 10°   120° TYP

Fig. 8–20 Detail of Stool Hole Pattern

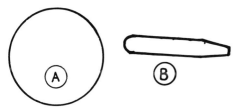
Fig. 8–18 Foot Stool

Fig. 8–21 Pattern for Potato Masher

Ⓐ Ⓑ

Fig. 8–19 Pattern for Stool

CONSTRUCTION

1. Cut seat **A** (Fig. 8–19). Drill hole pattern $\frac{1}{8}$ inch deep (Fig. 8–20). Then round edges.
2. Cut legs **B** to length. Taper one end to $\frac{1}{8}$ inch diameter, and round other end (Fig. 8–19).

ASSEMBLY

1. Glue legs **B** to seat **A** and assure seat is level.
2. Sand and stain desired color, and apply light coat of satin finish varnish.

POTATO MASHER

1. Cut a $\frac{5}{16}$ inch diameter dowel to $\frac{7}{8}$ inch long, and shape (Fig. 8–21).
2. Sand, and apply clear varnish.

SCOOP

CONSTRUCTION

1. Drill a $\frac{1}{4}$ inch diameter hole in the center of a $\frac{3}{8}$ inch diameter dowel. Then shape (Fig. 8–17).
2. Apply a light coat of clear varnish.

STOOL

MATERIALS

PART		DIMENSIONS	QUANTITY
A	Seat	$\frac{1}{4}$ × 1 dia.	1
B	Legs	$\frac{5}{32}$ dia. × $1\frac{1}{4}$	3

115

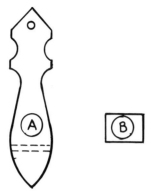

Fig. 8–22 Pattern for Wall Shelf

WALL SHELVES

MATERIALS

PART		DIMENSIONS
A	*Back*	$\frac{1}{16} \times \frac{1}{2} \times 1\frac{1}{2}$
B	*Shelf*	$\frac{1}{16} \times \frac{7}{32} \times \frac{3}{8}$

CONSTRUCTION

1. Cut back **A** to pattern (Fig. 8–22). Drill $\frac{3}{64}$ diameter hole at top.
2. Cut shelf **B** as shown in pattern, and round corners with sandpaper.
3. Sand parts smooth, and stain desired color.

ASSEMBLY

1. Glue shelf **B** to back **A**, as indicated by dotted lines.
2. Apply a light coat of satin finish varnish.

VIOLIN

The violin (Fig. 8–23) requires a considerable amount of time to build because of the amount of knife work involved. Basswood is recommended for this project because of the amount of carving required on the head scroll.

Fig. 8–23 Violin

CONSTRUCTION

1. Trace the outline (Fig. 8–24) on a $\frac{1}{4}$ inch thick piece of wood. With a jigsaw, cut pattern to the outside of the line. The shaping and sanding required will reduce all dimensions considerably.
2. Outline the neck extension on the body and assure symmetry with the body (Fig. 8–25).
3. Shape the neck as shown. The small projection on the neck is required to prevent the strings from resting on the body.
4. Very carefully drill two holes, $\frac{3}{32}$ inch deep, not through, on the right side of the neck (Fig. 8–25), using a #76 drill in a pin vise. Then drill two holes very carefully on the left side, spaced between those on the right side.

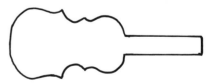

Fig. 8–24 Pattern for Violin Body

116

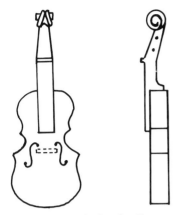

Fig. 8–25 Detail of Violin Shape

Fig. 8–26 Detail of Violin Scroll Head

 Fig. 8–27 Detail of Violin Peg

 Fig. 8–28 Pattern for Violin Bridge

Fig. 8–29 Pattern for Violin Bow

5. Shape head scroll of the violin (Fig. 8–26). The shape is as a canted spiral, like a spring: one to the right and one to the left.

6. Round top and bottom of the body (to create a convex-shaped body) by sanding with extra-fine sandpaper from the neck to the outside edge.

7. Sand entire piece smooth, and stain desired color. Gently rub stain with soft cotton cloth and apply second coat, removing the excess.

8. Drill two holes with #76 drill on each end of the S-shaped sound holes (Fig. 8–25). Trace the S curve using a fine-tipped pen with permanent ink.

9. Using #24 AWG copper wire, shape four pegs (Fig. 8–27; detail is not to scale). Flatten ends with a hammer and shape to pattern with a file. Then cut $\frac{3}{16}$ inch long. Paint flat black, allow to dry, and carefully install pegs into neck. It should be a tight fit, so use extra caution. Alternate position of pegs in head.

10. Cut the bridge (Fig. 8–28; detail is not to scale), from $\frac{1}{16}$ inch thick by $\frac{1}{8}$ inch high by $\frac{7}{32}$ inch wide at the base to approximately $\frac{1}{32}$ inch thick at the top. Make four equally spaced shallow grooves with a knife on the top for the strings. Sand lightly. Then glue in place, shown by dotted lines (Fig. 8–25).

11. Cut four lengths of #50 black thread for violin strings, and attach with glue on the neck next to respective pegs. Allow to dry. Apply a very small amount of glue on the neck projection, and attach the four strings equally spaced. When glue has dried, attach strings to respective grooves on bridge. Bring ends of strings together, and attach to end of the body with glue. Hold in position until glue has dried. Then trim ends with sharp knife.

12. Apply a light coat of satin finish spray varnish. Spray is recommended because violin is so small that brush strokes cannot be removed easily.

CONSTRUCTION (BOW)

1. Cut pattern of the bow (Fig. 8–29) from $\frac{1}{16}$ inch thick by $\frac{3}{16}$ inch wide by $2\frac{1}{4}$ inch long piece of basswood. Carefully round all edges, and shape handle.
2. Sand smooth, and stain dark walnut.
3. Carefully attach with glue three or four strands of beige or light brown thread, the finest grade you can find, to open side of bow. Trim excess with a razor blade.
4. Hold by threads and apply a spray coat of satin finish varnish.

GUITAR

The guitar is not as difficult to make as the violin because it is of a slightly more manageable size. Sugar pine or basswood may be used for carving (Fig. 8–30).

1. Trace pattern (Fig. 8–31) on a $\frac{7}{16}$ inch thick piece of wood. With a jigsaw cut out pattern, keeping to the outside of the line because of the shaping and sanding that will be required.
2. Outline the neck extension on the body to assure symmetry (Fig. 8–32).
3. Shape the neck as shown. The small projection in front of the head is required to prevent the strings from resting on the guitar body.
4. Carefully drill the six holes in the top of the head (Fig. 8–33; detail is not to scale) with a #60 drill. The hole pattern is staggered, like a full-size guitar,

Fig. 8–30 Guitars

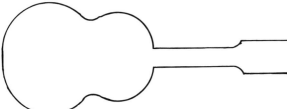

Fig. 8–31 Pattern for Guitar

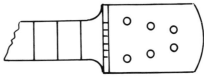

Fig. 8–33 Detail of Guitar Head

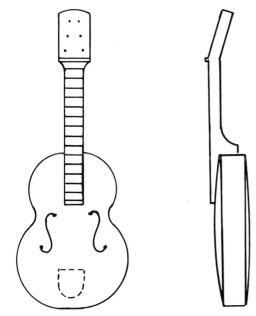

Fig. 8–32 Detail of Guitar Shape

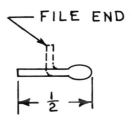

FILE END

Fig. 8–34 Detail of Guitar Peg

so the strings do not interfere with one another.

5. Cut the six string grooves in the projection on the neck, equally spaced (Fig. 8–33). Use a sharp knife or a fine three-cornered file.

6. The fret marks on the neck can be inserted with a sharp knife or a three-cornered file (Fig. 8–32).

7. Shape body to convex surface on both top and bottom, reducing the thickness of the outside edge.

8. Sand smooth the entire piece, and stain to desired color. Light oak or maple is recommended.

9. Drill two holes with #60 drill on each of the S-shaped sound holes (Fig. 8–32). Trace the S shape, and make a depression into the body with a wood-burning tip or a ballpoint pen tip.

10. Using #18 AWG copper wire, shape six pegs (Fig. 8–34; detail not to scale). Flatten one end with a hammer, and shape configuration with a file. Cut to ½ inch length, and bend at 90°. File cut end flat. Paint flat black, allow to dry, and install in drilled peg holes in the head. It should be a tight fit, so go slowly.

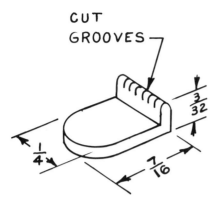

CUT GROOVES

Fig. 8–35 Detail of Guitar Bridge

11. Cut the bridge (Fig. 8–35; detail is not to scale) from a $\frac{3}{32}$ inch thick piece of wood by $\frac{1}{4}$ inch wide by $\frac{7}{16}$ inch long, and shape as shown. Make six equally spaced grooves on the top for the strings. Sand lightly, and paint flat black. Then glue into position shown by dotted lines (Fig. 8–32).

12. Cut six lengths of #50 black thread for the guitar strings. Tie with a knot to the protruding ends of the pegs. Apply a very small amount of glue on the neck projection, and attach the six strings in respective positions.

13. Place a small amount of glue on the bridge, and insert the six strings in respective positions. Bring ends together, and apply a weight or clamp (or a spring-type clothespin) to hold strings in position until the glue has dried.

14. Apply a light coat of satin finish spray varnish. When varnish is dry, buff with fine grade of steel wool.

LAMPS

Included in this book are plans for a desk lamp and a table lamp (Fig. 8–36), which are easy to make with a wood lathe.

Fig. 8–36 Lamp Assortment

120

MATERIALS (DESK LAMP)

PART		DIMENSIONS
A	*Base*	$\frac{1}{2}$ dia. dowel $\times$ $\frac{7}{8}$
B	*Globe*	$\frac{3}{4}$ dia. fishing bobber
C	*Chimney*	$\frac{3}{16}$ dia. $\times$ $\frac{5}{8}$ plastic tubing

CONSTRUCTION

1. Cut base **A** to pattern (Fig. 8–37). Stain or paint desired color. Then apply a thin coat of varnish.
2. Cut globe **B** from one half of a fishing bobber.
3. Cut chimney **C** to length from $\frac{3}{16}$ inch diameter plastic tubing.

ASSEMBLY

1. Glue globe **B** to base **A** (Fig. 8–38).
2. Glue chimney **C** to inside of globe **A**.

MATERIALS (TABLE LAMP)

PART		DIMENSIONS
A	*Base*	$\frac{5}{8}$ dia. $\times$ $1\frac{3}{16}$
B	*Globe*	$1\frac{1}{4}$ dia. fishing bobber
C	*Chimney*	$\frac{1}{4}$ dia. plastic tubing

CONSTRUCTION

1. Cut base **A** to pattern (Fig. 8–39). Stain or paint desired color. Then apply a thin finish coat.
2. Cut globe **B** from one half of a fishing bobber.
3. Cut chimney **C** to length from $\frac{1}{4}$ inch diameter plastic tubing.

ASSEMBLY

1. Glue globe **B** to base **A** (Fig. 8–40).
2. Glue chimney **C** to inside of globe **A**.

Fig. 8–37 *Pattern for Desk Lamp*

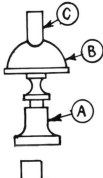

Fig. 8–38 *Assembling Desk Lamp*

Fig. 8–39 *Pattern for Table Lamp*

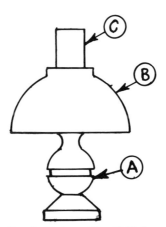

Fig. 8–40 *Assembling Table Lamp*

PICTURES

Unfinished picture-frame molding is available in many shapes and widths suitable for any decor. Better craft shops, hobby stores, and specialty shops carry an assortment of various styles.

The picture frames shown in Figs. 8–41 and 8–42 were cut from picture frame molding. The best results for a neatly cut 45° corner can be obtained with a miter box and razor blade (Fig. 8–43). (Miter box has sides removed to facilitate cutting.) Use a single-edge razor blade for cutting the picture-frame molding; because the molding is fragile, it has a tendency to chip with a fine-toothed saw.

The glass was cut from thin clear plastic, such as the type used for credit card holders or photo albums. Thin cardboard was used for the backing.

Suggested sources for subject material include commemorative issues of postage stamps, catalogs from department stores that specialize in original art, and furniture ads in magazines. Or try your hand at making your own. Sketch an outline on watercolor paper using a drafting pen with a 00 or 000 pen point (see Fig. 2–3) and waterproof ink. Then watercolor using acrylic artist paints thinned to watercolor consistency.

Pen-and-ink sketches can provide some very interesting pictures in miniature, from copies of the great masters to your own originals.

Fig. 8–41 Assortment of Pictures

Fig. 8–42 Mirror and Picture Assortment

Fig. 8–43 Cutting Picture Frame

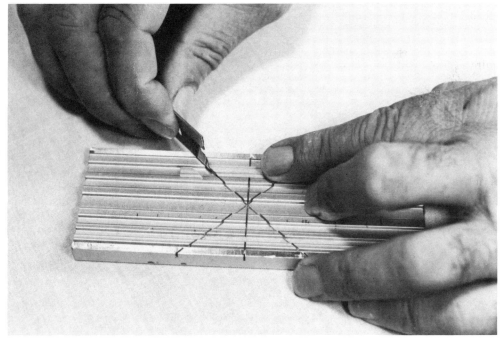

Fig. 8-44 Duck Decoys

DUCK DECOY

The duck decoys (Fig. 8-44) are made from sugar pine rather than basswood because of the thickness of the wood required. The pattern for these decoys is shown in Fig. 8-45. The decoy is shaped with a knife (Fig. 8-46), and then sanded smooth. Stain the decoy to the desired color. Then paint the beak and eyes with a flat black paint. When paint is dry, apply a coat of satin finish spray varnish. Then buff lightly with steel wool.

Fig. 8-46 Carving a Duck Decoy

Fig. 8-45 Pattern for Duck Decoys

CANDLE BOX

MATERIALS

PART		DIMENSIONS	QUANTITY
A	Back	$\frac{1}{16} \times \frac{5}{8} \times 1\frac{3}{4}$	1
B	Side	$\frac{1}{16} \times \frac{3}{8} \times 1\frac{3}{16}$	2
C	Front	$\frac{1}{16} \times \frac{5}{8} \times \frac{15}{16}$	1
D	Bottom	$\frac{1}{16} \times \frac{3}{8} \times \frac{1}{2}$	1

124

Fig. 8–47 Candle Box

CONSTRUCTION

1. Cut the back **A** with a jigsaw (Fig. 8–48). Then drill a $\frac{3}{64}$ inch diameter hole on center as indicated. Sand saw-cut edges smooth.
2. Cut two sides **B** to pattern (Fig. 8–48).
3. Cut front **C** to pattern (Fig. 8–48). Then sand edges.
4. Cut bottom **D** to size, and sand edges.
5. Stain parts to desired color.

ASSEMBLY

1. Glue the two sides **B** to front side of back **A** and flush with edges (Fig. 8–49).

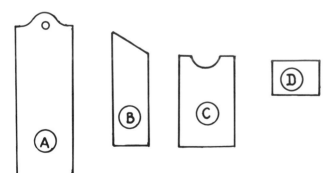

Fig. 8–48 Candle Box Pattern

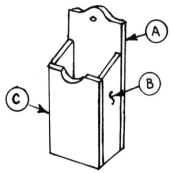

Fig. 8–49 *Assembling the Candle Box*

2. Glue bottom **D** flush with back **A** and sides **B**.
3. Glue front **C** flush to sides **B** and flush with bottom **D**.
4. Apply a light coat of semigloss varnish.

BED STEP

MATERIALS

PART		DIMENSIONS	QUANTITY
A	Top	$\frac{3}{32} \times \frac{3}{4} \times 1\frac{1}{2}$	1
B	Leg	$\frac{3}{32} \times \frac{5}{8} \times \frac{3}{4}$	2
C	Brace	$\frac{1}{16} \times \frac{5}{16} \times \frac{1}{18}$	1

Fig. 8–50 *Bed Step*

CONSTRUCTION

1. Cut top **A** to pattern (Fig. 8–51). Then locate position of the hand grip hole, and drill a $\frac{3}{32}$ diameter hole on each end, removing the web between with a knife. Round corners, and sand smooth with sandpaper.
2. Cut two legs **B** to pattern (Fig. 8–51). Then sand smooth.
3. Cut brace **C** to dimensions. Then sand edges.
4. Stain parts to desired color.

ASSEMBLY

1. Glue brace **C** on center between legs **B** (Fig. 8–52).
2. Glue top **A** centered on legs **B**.
3. Apply a thin coat of satin finish spray varnish.

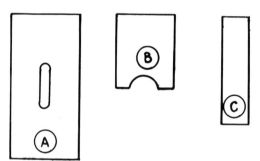

Fig. 8–51 *Bed Step Pattern*

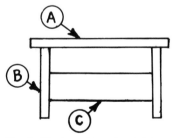

Fig. 8–52 *Assembling the Bed Step*

TOWEL RACK

MATERIALS

PART		DIMENSIONS	QUANTITY
A	*Back*	$\frac{1}{16} \times 1\frac{1}{8} \times 1\frac{11}{16}$	1
B	*Side*	$\frac{1}{16} \times \frac{7}{16} \times 1$	2
C	*Shelf*	$\frac{1}{16} \times \frac{3}{8} \times 1\frac{11}{16}$	1
D	*Bar*	$\frac{1}{8}$ dia. dowel $\times$ $1\frac{11}{16}$	1
E	*Handle*	$\frac{1}{8}$ dia. dowel $\times$ $\frac{5}{8}$	2

CONSTRUCTION

1. Cut back **A** to pattern (Fig. 8–54) with a jigsaw. Drill $\frac{3}{64}$ inch diameter hole in location shown. Sand edges smooth.
2. Cut two sides **B** to pattern (Fig. 8–54) with a jigsaw. Then drill a $\frac{1}{16}$ inch diameter hole through to location indicated.
3. Cut shelf **C** to dimensions.
4. Cut bar **D** to length. Then drill $\frac{1}{16}$ inch diameter hole in each end $\frac{3}{32}$ inch deep.
5. Cut two handles **E** to length. Then reduce one end to $\frac{1}{16}$ inch diameter.
6. Stain parts to desired color.

Fig. 8–53 Towel Rack

ASSEMBLY

1. Glue sides **B** flush with edges of back **A** (Fig. 8–55).
2. Glue shelf **C** to back and sides in position shown.

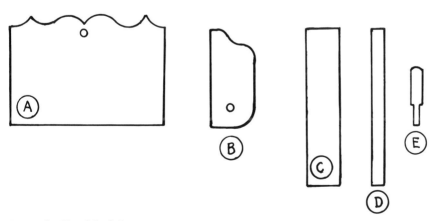

Fig. 8–54 Towel Rack Pattern

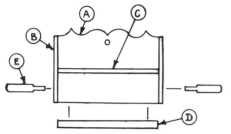

Fig. 8–55 Assembling the Towel Rack

3. Trim length of bar **D** to fit loosely between the sides **B**.
4. Attach handles **E** to bar through the hole in the sides **B**, but do not glue in place.
5. Apply a light coat of satin finish varnish.

MIRROR FRAME

MATERIALS

PART		DIMENSIONS	QUANTITY
A	Back	$\frac{3}{32} \times 1\frac{3}{8} \times 2\frac{7}{16}$	1
B	Frame	$\frac{1}{32} \times \frac{7}{8} \times 1\frac{3}{4}$	1
C	Mirror	$\frac{3}{32} \times \frac{11}{16} \times 1\frac{9}{16}$	1

CONSTRUCTION

1. Cut back **A** to pattern (Fig. 8–57) with a jigsaw. Drill $\frac{3}{64}$ inch diameter hole on center as shown.
2. Cut frame **B** to pattern (Fig. 8–57) with a jigsaw. Then round edges with sandpaper.
3. Cut mirror **C** to size with a glass cutter.
4. Stain back and frame to desired color.

Fig. 8–56 Mirror Frame

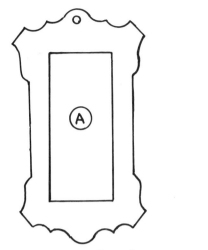

Fig. 8–57 *Mirror Frame Pattern*

ASSEMBLY

1. Center frame **B** on back **A**, and attach with glue.
2. Apply a light coat of satin finish varnish.
3. Insert mirror **C** into back assembly, and apply a small amount of glue to edge of mirror.

SCONCES

MATERIALS

PART		DIMENSIONS
A	*Back*	$\frac{3}{32} \times \frac{11}{32} \times 1\frac{5}{16}$
B	*Cup*	$\frac{3}{32}$ dia. hollow brass rivet $\times \frac{1}{4}$ long
C	*Disc*	$\frac{1}{4}$ dia. brass shim stock
D	*Candle*	$\frac{3}{32}$ dia. dowel $\times \frac{3}{4}$ long
E	*Bracket*	24 gauge brass wire $\times 1\frac{1}{4}$ long

CONSTRUCTION

1. Cut back **A** to pattern (Fig. 8–58), and drill $\frac{1}{32}$ inch diameter hole at location indicated.

2. The disc **C** can be made from .002 or .003 thick brass shim stock. Shape with tin snip or old paper punch.
3. Cut candle **D** to length, and shape (Fig. 8–58). Paint candle with flat white paint.
4. Form bracket **E** by wrapping around a $\frac{1}{4}$ inch diameter dowel to pattern (Fig. 8–59).

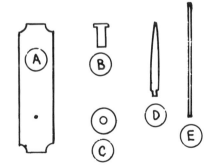

Fig. 8–58 *Sconce Pattern*

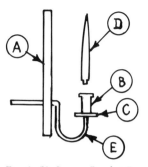

Fig. 8–59 Sconce Bracket Pattern

ASSEMBLY

1. Assemble wire bracket **E** through disc **C** and into cup **B** on center. Then solder in place (Fig. 8–59).

2. Thread end of wire bracket **E** into back **A**. Then form flat against back **A**.

3. Glue candle **D** into cup **B**.

PAN RACK

MATERIALS

PART		DIMENSIONS	QUANTITY
A	*Back*	$\frac{3}{32} \times \frac{1}{2} \times 3$	1
B	*Peg*	$\frac{1}{16}$ dia. dowel $\times \frac{5}{16}$ long	4

CONSTRUCTION

1. Cut back **A** to pattern (Fig. 8–61) with a jigsaw. Drill $\frac{1}{16}$ inch diameter holes at a 5° angle at locations indicated. Sand edges smooth.

Fig. 8–60 Pan Rack

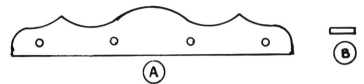

Fig. 8–61 Pan Rack Back Pattern

2. Cut four pegs **B** to length, and round ends.
3. Stain parts to desired color.

ASSEMBLY

1. Glue pegs **B** into back **A**.
2. Apply a light coat of satin finish varnish. Buff lightly with steel wool.

HEARTH BROOM

To make the hearth broom handle, cut a $\frac{5}{32}$ inch diameter dowel $1\frac{3}{4}$ inch long, and shape to pattern (Fig. 8–63). Stain to desired color. Cut bristles from a dis-

Fig. 8–62 Hearth Broom

carded paint brush $1\frac{5}{8}$ inch long, and attach with glue to small end of the handle. Then wrap with brown thread.

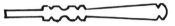

Fig. 8–63 Hearth Broom Handle Pattern

CANDLE HOLDERS

MATERIALS

PART		DIMENSIONS
A	*Base*	$\frac{9}{16}$ dia. × $\frac{1}{4}$ long
B	*Cup*	$\frac{3}{16}$ dia. dowel × $\frac{9}{16}$ long
C	*Candle*	$\frac{3}{32}$ dia. dowel × 1 long

CONSTRUCTION

1. The base **A** can be shaped from a $\frac{1}{4}$ inch thick piece of basswood. Drill a $\frac{3}{16}$ inch diameter hole in the center (Fig. 8–65). Or use a #0 size faucet washer, which has the same dimensions.
2. Cut the cup **B** to length, and shape (Fig. 8–65). Drill a $\frac{1}{16}$ inch diameter hole in the end for the candle.
3. Cut the candle **C** to length, and shape as shown. Sand and paint flat white.

ASSEMBLY

1. Glue cup **B** into base **A**.
2. Paint assembly with gold hobby paint.
3. Glue candle **C** into cup **B**.

131

Fig. 8–64 Candle Holders

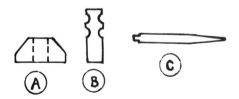

Fig. 8–65 Candle Holders Pattern

COFFEE GRINDER

MATERIALS

PART		DIMENSIONS	QUANTITY
A	Side	$\frac{3}{32} \times \frac{5}{8} \times \frac{9}{16}$	2
B	Base	$\frac{3}{32} \times \frac{3}{4} \times \frac{3}{4}$	1
C	Back	$\frac{3}{32} \times \frac{1}{2} \times \frac{9}{16}$	1

D	*Front*	$\frac{1}{16} \times \frac{1}{4} \times \frac{11}{16}$	1
E	*Top*	$\frac{3}{32} \times \frac{3}{4} \times \frac{3}{4}$	1
F	*Crown*	$\frac{3}{32} \times \frac{7}{16}$ diameter	1
G	*Shaft*	$\frac{3}{32}$ dia. dowel $\times \frac{1}{2}$	1
H	*Hub*	$\frac{5}{32}$ dia. dowel $\times \frac{1}{8}$	1
I	*Crank*	$\frac{3}{32} \times \frac{1}{4} \times \frac{7}{8}$	1
J	*Knob*	$\frac{5}{32}$ dia. dowel $\times$ $\frac{3}{16}$	1
K	*Drawer Front*	$\frac{1}{16} \times \frac{9}{32} \times \frac{11}{16}$	1
L	*Drawer Side*	$\frac{1}{32} \times \frac{1}{4} \times \frac{17}{32}$	1
M	*Drawer Back*	$\frac{1}{32} \times \frac{1}{4} \times \frac{3}{8}$	1
N	*Drawer Bottom*	$\frac{1}{32} \times \frac{3}{8} \times \frac{1}{2}$	1
O	*Handle*	drawer pull (purchased)	1
P	*Drawer Pull*	Bead and nail	1 ea.

CONSTRUCTION

1. Cut back **C** to dimensions, and notch top edge (Fig. 8–67).

Fig. 8–66 Coffee Grinder

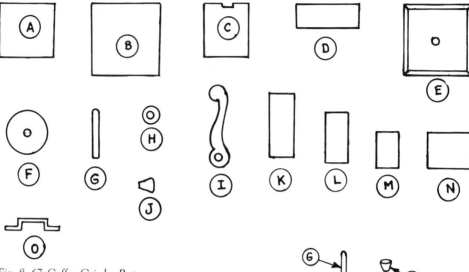

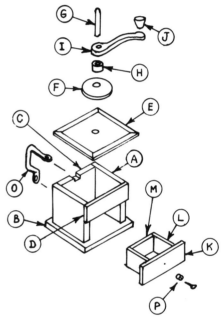

Fig. 8–67 Coffee Grinder Pattern

2. Cut top **E** to size. Then bevel top edge at 45° with sandpaper. Paint flat black.

3. Cut crown **F** to size, and round top side. Drill a $\frac{3}{32}$ inch diameter hole through center. Paint flat black.

4. Cut shaft **G** to length, and round ends with sandpaper. Paint flat black.

5. Cut hub **H** to length, and drill $\frac{3}{32}$ inch diameter hole through center. Paint flat black.

6. Cut crank **I** to pattern (Fig. 8–67). Drill $\frac{3}{32}$ inch diameter hole in location shown, and round edges with sandpaper. Paint flat black.

7. Cut knob **J** to shape (Fig. 8–67).

8. Cut remaining parts to dimension. Then sand and stain to desired color all unpainted parts.

ASSEMBLY

1. Glue sides **A** to back **C**. Then center parts on base **B** (Fig. 8–68).

2. Glue front **D** in position shown.

Fig. 8–68 Assembling the Coffee Grinder

3. Shape handle **O** as shown and attach with nails to back **C**.

4. Glue top **E** to sides **A** and to back **C**.

5. Glue shaft **G** to top **E**, flush with inside, and glue crown **F** to shaft.

6. Glue hub **H** in place.

134

7. Glue knob **J** to crank **I**. Then place on shaft **G** but *do not* glue in place.

8. Glue drawer bottom **N** and drawer sides **L** flush with bottom edge of drawer front **K**.

9. Glue drawer back **M** flush with sides **L**.

10. Attach bead and nail **P** to drawer front **K** (Fig. 8–68).

11. Apply a light coat of satin finish varnish.

QUILT HOLDER

MATERIALS

PART		DIMENSIONS	QUANTITY
A	*Brace*	$\frac{1}{8} \times \frac{9}{16} \times 1\frac{1}{2}$	2
B	*Leg*	$\frac{1}{8} \times \frac{5}{8} \times 1\frac{1}{2}$	2
C	*Support*	$\frac{1}{8}$ dia. dowel $\times 1\frac{7}{16}$	4
D	*Rods*	$\frac{3}{32}$ dia. dowel $\times 2$	4

CONSTRUCTION

1. Cut two braces **A** with a jigsaw to pattern (Fig. 8–70). Drill three $\frac{1}{16}$ inch diameter holes in side but not through. Drill two $\frac{1}{16}$ inch diameter holes on the bottom edge, as indicated by the dotted lines.

2. Cut two legs **B** with a jigsaw to pattern

Fig. 8–69 *Quilt Holder*

(Fig. 8–70). Drill one $\frac{1}{16}$ inch diameter hole in side but not through. Drill two $\frac{1}{16}$ inch diameter holes on the top edge, as indicated by the dotted lines, to match the holes in brace **A**.

3. Cut four supports **C** to length. Then shape with a knife to pattern (Fig. 8–70). Taper ends to $\frac{1}{16}$ inch diameter.

4. Cut four rods **D** to length. Then reduce ends to $\frac{1}{16}$ inch diameter (Fig. 8–70).

5. Sand and stain parts to desired color.

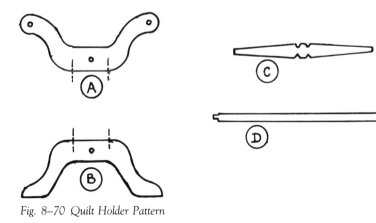

Fig. 8–70 *Quilt Holder Pattern*

ASSEMBLY

1. Glue two supports **C** to each brace **A** and leg **B**.
2. Glue three rods **D** between the two braces **A**.
3. Glue one rod **D** between the two legs **B**.
4. Apply a light coat of satin finish var-

nish. Buff with steel wool, and apply second coat if desired.

BED WARMER

MATERIALS

PART		DIMENSIONS
A	*Pan*	1 dia. $\times \frac{7}{16}$
B	*Handle*	$\frac{5}{32}$ dia. dowel $\times 2\frac{1}{2}$

Fig. 8–71 Bed Warmer

136

CONSTRUCTION

1. Cut pan **A** to pattern (Fig. 8–72). Drill $\frac{3}{32}$ inch diameter hole $\frac{1}{4}$ inch deep. Cut groove all around. Then round edges with sandpaper and paint with brass or antique gold hobby paint.
2. Cut handle **B** to pattern (Fig. 8–72). Sand smooth, and stain to desired color.

ASSEMBLY

1. Glue handle **B** into the pan **A**.
2. Apply a light coat of semigloss varnish.

PIPE RACK

MATERIALS

PART		DIMENSIONS	QUANTITY
A	Side	$\frac{1}{16} \times \frac{5}{16} \times \frac{3}{4}$	2
B	Top	$\frac{1}{16} \times \frac{5}{32} \times \frac{11}{16}$	1
C	Bottom	$\frac{1}{16} \times \frac{5}{16} \times \frac{11}{16}$	1

CONSTRUCTION

1. Cut two sides **A** to pattern (Fig. 8–74).
2. Cut top **B** to pattern (Fig. 8–74).

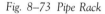

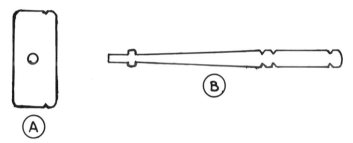

Fig. 8–72 Bed Warmer Pattern

Fig. 8–73 Pipe Rack

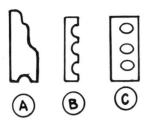

Fig. 8–74 Pipe Rack Pattern

3. Cut bottom **C** to pattern (Fig. 8–74). (Use gouge to form recesses for pipes.)
4. Sand parts smooth, and stain.

ASSEMBLY

1. Glue bottom **C** to sides **A**, $\frac{1}{8}$ inch from end.

2. Glue top **B** to sides **A**, flush with back edge and $\frac{1}{8}$ inch from end.
3. Apply a light coat of satin finish varnish.

PIPES

Use $\frac{1}{8}$-inch-thick stock, $\frac{3}{16}$ wide and $\frac{3}{4}$ inch long. To shape pipe, start by drilling $\frac{1}{16}$ inch diameter hole $\frac{1}{8}$ inch deep in one side. Then shape (Fig. 8–75).

Fig. 8–75 Pipes

Fig. 8–76 Wooden Bowls and Dishes

WOODEN BOWLS AND DISHES

For a symmetrical shape and uniform wall thickness, a lathe is necessary to turn the bowls. A metal cutting lathe with a three- or four-jaw chuck is ideal; a wood lathe with a faceplate can be used with excellent results. The largest bowl shown is one inch in diameter; the smallest is $\frac{5}{8}$ inch. Try to maintain a wall and bottom thickness of $\frac{3}{32}$ inch. Thinner walls and bottoms have a tendency to break easily.

CHAPTER 9

Building the Cape Cod Dollhouse

The dollhouse shown in Fig. 9–1 is a versatile design, allowing several options for completion at various stages.

Option 1. The dollhouse can be built as

shown with the windows, dormers, siding, shingles, and front door.

Option 2. The dollhouse may be built without the dormers and windows, and com-

Fig. 9–1 Completed Dollhouse

pleted as shown in Fig. 9–2. This will reduce the building time considerably and allow maximum flexibility in furniture arrangement.

Option 3. The stairwell may be eliminated, and four wall partitions may be installed to give six rooms approximately 10 x 11 inches each.

Available time and personal preference will dictate which option you choose.

HOUSE FRAME

The dollhouse is constructed with a false front door to maximize the interior wall space for furniture arrangement. The basic house pattern (Fig. 9–3) may be obtained from a $\frac{3}{8}$ inch $\times$ 4 foot $\times$ 4 foot sheet of plywood plus a few scrap pieces of lumber. The materials list is for the basic structure only. Material for the stairs, windows, dormers, and exterior

Fig. 9–2 Basic Dollhouse Structure

door will be described later as they are added to the basic structure.

MATERIALS

PART		DIMENSIONS
A	Front Roof	$12\frac{3}{4} \times 31\frac{1}{2}$
B	Front Wall	12×30
C	First floor	$11 \times 29\frac{1}{4}$
D	Right Side	$11 \times 19\frac{3}{4}$
E	Left Side	$11 \times 19\frac{3}{4}$
F	Second floor	$11 \times 29\frac{1}{4}$
G	Back Roof	$5 \times 31\frac{1}{2}$
H	Bedroom Wall	$4\frac{1}{2} \times 10\frac{5}{8}$
I	Living Room Wall	$4 \times 8\frac{3}{8}$
J	Partition Wall	$3\frac{1}{4} \times 8\frac{3}{8}$
K	Living Room Wall	$4\frac{1}{8} \times 8\frac{3}{8}$
L	Kitchen Wall	$7 \times 8\frac{3}{8}$
M	Bedroom Wall	$2\frac{1}{2} \times 5\frac{3}{4}$
N	Bedroom Wall	$4\frac{3}{8} \times 6\frac{1}{4}$

Layout pattern on plywood and label each piece before cutting with table saw or saber saw. Allow for saw cut width.

CONSTRUCTION

1. If dormers are included, cut window opening in roof **A**, as shown in the pattern (Fig. 9–3). For ease in cutting window openings, drill $\frac{3}{8}$ inch diameter hole. Then use saber saw to cut out window opening.

2. Cut front wall **B**, and bevel top edge at 45° to match end pieces. Cut window openings to full width and length with sharp square corners, as windows are made for a snug fit.

142

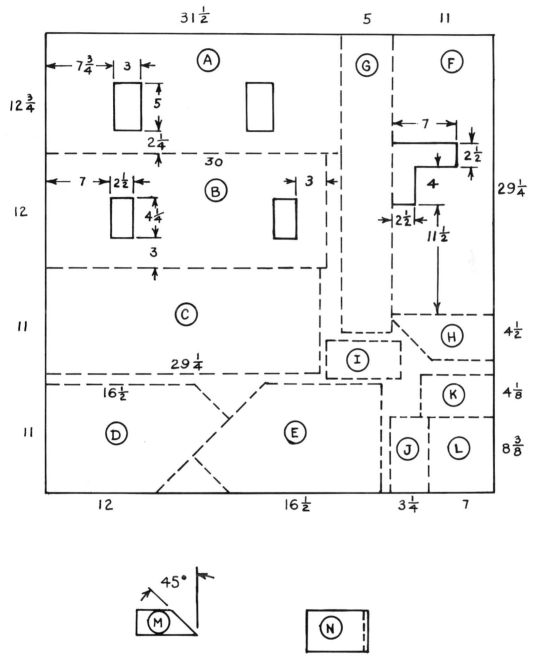

Fig. 9–3 Pattern for Dollhouse

143

3. Cut bedroom walls **H**, **M**, and **N** to length after installing the staircase.

4. Cut remaining pieces and sand sawcuts.

ASSEMBLY

1. Dry fit front wall **B**, right and left sides **D** and **E**, first and second floors **C** and **F**, and front roof **A** only. Then assemble (Fig. 9–4).

2. Fasten first floor **C** to right and left sides **D** and **E** with glue and brads.

3. Space second floor **F** $8\frac{3}{8}$ inches above the first floor, with stairwell opening facing the front of the house. Nail and glue to sides **D** and **E**.

4. Center front wall **B**, and attach flush to edges of sides, **D** and **E** and first floor **F** with glue and brads.

STAIRWAY

All fourteen stair risers are $\frac{5}{8}$ inch high. To form step supports for the stairs, rip $\frac{1}{8}$ inch thick by $\frac{5}{8}$ wide strips from scrap lumber and lay out pattern (Figs. 9–5 and 9–6). (Use Fig. 9–7 as reference only.)

1. Start at top of kitchen wall **L** and measure down $\frac{1}{4}$ inch. Then measure $\frac{5}{8}$ inch from the side (Fig. 9–5). This will locate step #1. At $\frac{5}{8}$ inch spacing, add steps 2 through 7.

2. Step 8 is the landing. Extend step support to within $\frac{1}{8}$ inch from edge of wall, as shown.

3. Locate edge of kitchen wall on front wall, and align perpendicular with stairwell opening on second floor. This will

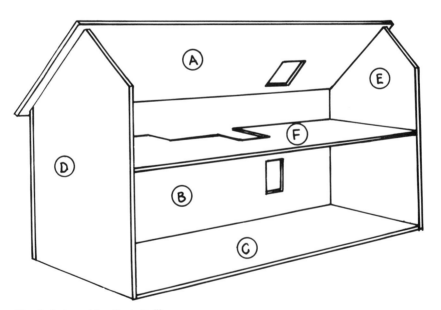

Fig. 9–4 Assembling Basic Dollhouse

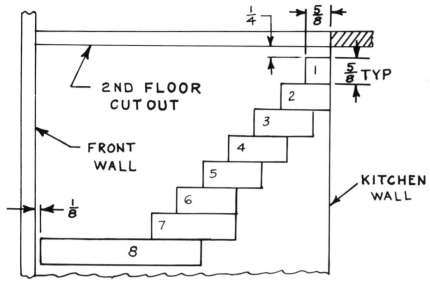

Fig. 9–5 *Layout of Stairs on Kitchen Wall*

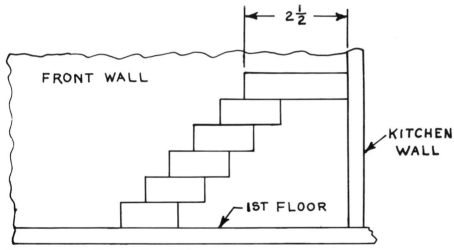

Fig. 9–6 *Layout of Stairs on Front Wall*

locate stair landing on the front wall. (See Fig. 9–6.) Cut landing support $2\frac{1}{2}$ inches long as indicated, and continue with step supports at $\frac{5}{8}$ inch spacing to floor.

4. Make mirror image of the previously constructed step supports on living room walls **I** and **K**.

5. Assemble walls **I**, **J**, **K**, and **L** (Fig. 9–8) with glue and brads.

145

Fig. 9–7 Stairwell Layout

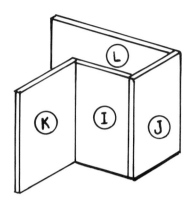

Fig. 9–8 Staircase Assembly

STAIR TREADS AND RISERS

1. Cut risers from material $\frac{3}{32}$ inch thick by $\frac{5}{8}$ inch wide by $2\frac{1}{2}$ inch long. Sand smooth, and stain desired color. Then install on the upper level of stairs.

2. Cut stair treads from material $\frac{3}{32}$ inch thick by $\frac{3}{4}$ inch wide by $2\frac{1}{2}$ inch long. Sand smooth, and stain desired color. Then install on the upper level of stairs.

3. Place stairwell in position on first floor (Fig. 9–9).

4. Add remaining risers and stair treads as required.

5. For the landing, cut a piece of lumber $\frac{3}{32}$ inch thick (Fig. 9–10). Sand, stain, and glue in place.

BEDROOM WALLS

1. Attach back roof **G** to sides **D** and **E** and front roof **A** with glue and brads (Fig. 9–9).

2. Fit and cut bedroom walls **H**, **M**, and **N** to length and install (Fig. 9–9).

DORMERS

If you wish to avoid the time and effort required to build dormers, you can purchase them ready-made at most hobby and craft stores. The dormers shown can be constructed from available scrap plywood.

MATERIALS

Dimensions are for $\frac{3}{8}$ inch plywood.

PART		DIMENSIONS	QUANTITY
A	Side	$3\frac{7}{8} \times 3\frac{7}{8}$	2
B	Ceiling	$3 \times 3\frac{7}{8}$	1
C	Front	$3\frac{3}{4} \times 6\frac{1}{8}$	1
D	Roof (right and left)	$3\frac{1}{2} \times 7$	2

CONSTRUCTION

1. Cut two sides **A** to dimension and at 45°, as shown.

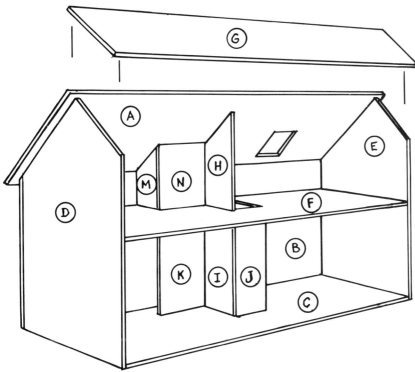

Fig. 9–9 Assembling Stairwell and Roof

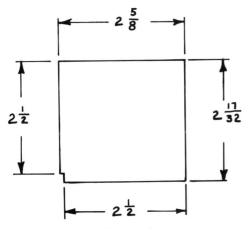

Fig. 9–10 Detail of Stair Landing

2. Cut ceiling **B** to length, and bevel end at 45°.

3. Cut front **C** as shown, cut out window opening, and bevel bottom edge at 45°.

4. Cut roof **D**, one right hand and one left hand. The angle on the back edge will be a compound 45° angle cut. Variations in dimensions of the previously cut pieces will determine what this angle is. Cut and fit to determine a good fit. The roof line need not match exactly, as small gaps will be concealed by the shingles that are added later.

5. Sand saw-cut edges on all pieces.

ASSEMBLY

1. Attach sides and ceiling **A** and **B** with glue and brads (Fig. 9–12).

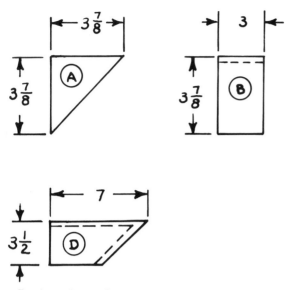

Fig. 9–11 Pattern for Dormer

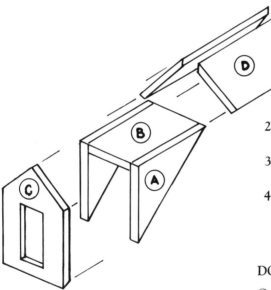

Fig. 9–12 Assembling Dormer

2. Attach front **C** flush with edges of both sides **A** with glue and brads.
3. Assemble both roof sections **D**, and trim to fit if necessary. Then glue in place.
4. Center dormer assembly over opening in front roof, and attach with glue. Nail in place.

DORMER WINDOWS

Once the dormers are in place, the windows can be added.

MATERIALS ($\frac{1}{8}$ inch thick material)

PART	DIMENSIONS	QUANTITY
A *Casing*	$\frac{3}{8} \times 1\frac{1}{2}$	2

B	Vertical Casing	$\frac{3}{8} \times 2\frac{7}{8}$	2
C	Horizontal Divider	$\frac{1}{8} \times 1\frac{1}{4}$	1
D	Vertical Divider	$\frac{3}{32} \times 1\frac{3}{8}$	2
E	Top Frame	$\frac{3}{8} \times 2\frac{1}{8}$	1
F	Side Frame	$\frac{3}{8} \times 3$	2
G	Bottom Frame	$\frac{1}{2} \times 2\frac{1}{8}$	1

CONSTRUCTION

1. Cut all parts to dimensions (Fig. 9–13).

ASSEMBLY

1. Glue together casings **A** and **B** (Fig. 9–14).
2. Glue dividers **C** and **D** in place.
3. Add outside frame parts **E**, **F**, and **G**, allowing $\frac{1}{16}$ clearance with casing, as indicated.

4. Dry fit assembled window with dormer but do not glue in place. Applying siding and painting will be simplified if window is removable.

FIRST-FLOOR WINDOWS

MATERIALS ($\frac{1}{8}$-inch-thick material)

PART		DIMENSIONS	QUANTITY
A	Vertical Casing	$\frac{3}{8} \times 4$	2
B	Horizontal Casing	$\frac{3}{8} \times 2\frac{1}{2}$	2
C	Center Crossbar	$\frac{3}{16} \times 2\frac{1}{2}$	1
D	Crossbar	$\frac{3}{32} \times 2\frac{1}{4}$	2
E	Vertical Divider	$\frac{3}{32} \times \frac{29}{32}$	4
F	Horizontal Frame	$\frac{1}{2} \times 3\frac{3}{8}$	2
G	Vertical Frame	$\frac{1}{2} \times 4\frac{1}{8}$	2

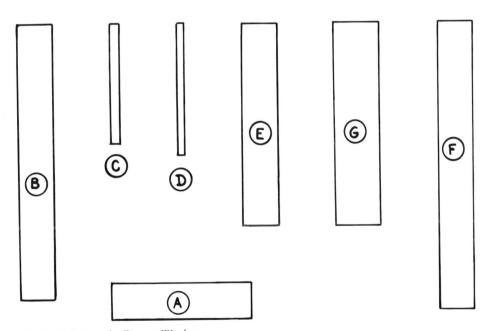

Fig. 9–13 Pattern for Dormer Window

149

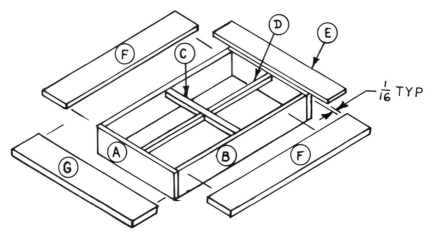

Fig. 9–14 Assembling Dormer Window

CONSTRUCTION

1. Cut vertical casing **A**, and notch in the center to accept crossbar **D** (Fig. 9–15).
2. Cut remaining parts to dimensions indicated, and sand lightly.

ASSEMBLY

1. Assemble in same manner as dormer windows. (Refer to Fig. 9–14.) Glue center crossbar **C** to vertical casing **A**.
2. Attach horizontal casings **B** to ends of vertical casing **A**.
3. Insert one crossbar **D** halfway below center crossbar **C**.
4. Attach horizontal and vertical frame **F** and **G** to casing at $\frac{1}{16}$ inch spacing.
5. Fit vertical divider **E** on center, and attach with glue. To facilitate painting and siding, do not glue in place.

EXTERIOR DOOR

The exterior door is a false door only appearing on the outside of the house. This is to allow maximum furniture rearrangement in the living room.

MATERIALS

PART		DIMENSIONS	QUANTITY
A	Frame	$\frac{1}{8} \times \frac{1}{2} \times 7\frac{1}{4}$	2
B	Sill	$\frac{1}{16} \times \frac{1}{4} \times$ $3\frac{9}{16}$	1
C	Crossbrace	$\frac{3}{32} \times \frac{1}{2} \times 2$	3
D	Door Edge	$\frac{3}{32} \times \frac{1}{2} \times$ $6\frac{3}{4}$	2
E	Base	$\frac{3}{32} \times \frac{3}{8} \times$ $3\frac{1}{16}$	1
F	Header	$\frac{1}{8} \times \frac{1}{2} \times$ $4\frac{1}{16}$	1
G	Top Panel	$\frac{3}{32} \times \frac{3}{4} \times \frac{7}{8}$	2
H	Mid Panel	$\frac{3}{32} \times \frac{3}{4} \times$ $1\frac{5}{16}$	2
I	Bottom Panel	$\frac{3}{32} \times \frac{3}{4} \times$ $2\frac{1}{8}$	2

CONSTRUCTION

1. Cut sill **B** to pattern (Fig. 9–16).
2. Cut panels **G**, **H**, and **I** as shown in pattern. Then bevel front edges with sandpaper. Cut remaining parts.

ASSEMBLY

1. Locate frame **A** one inch from right window opening and flush with bottom of first floor. Then glue in place.

2. Assemble remaining pieces (Fig. 9–17 and 9–18).

SIDING

If siding is desired, start by placing caps on the front corners of the dollhouse (Fig. 9–19). Cut $\frac{1}{8}$ inch thick lumber into $\frac{7}{16}$ inch wide strips for the front and back and $\frac{3}{8}$ inch wide strips for the sides. Apply strips from the base to the roof. Nail and glue in place (Fig. 9–20).

CUTTING THE SIDING

Use a standard $\frac{3}{4}$ inch thick board approximately 3 feet long. Rip this into $\frac{1}{32}$ inch wide strips. (A smooth finish cut can be obtained using a plywood cutting blade.) Start at the base of the house and mark $\frac{1}{2}$ inch increments up to the roof on the corner caps on both ends. With a framing square or a straight piece of lumber, connect the marks with a straight line, marking edges of door and window frames. Then place first course

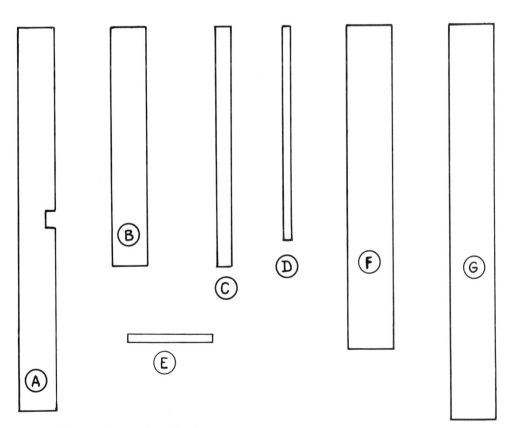

Fig. 9–15 Pattern for First Floor Windows

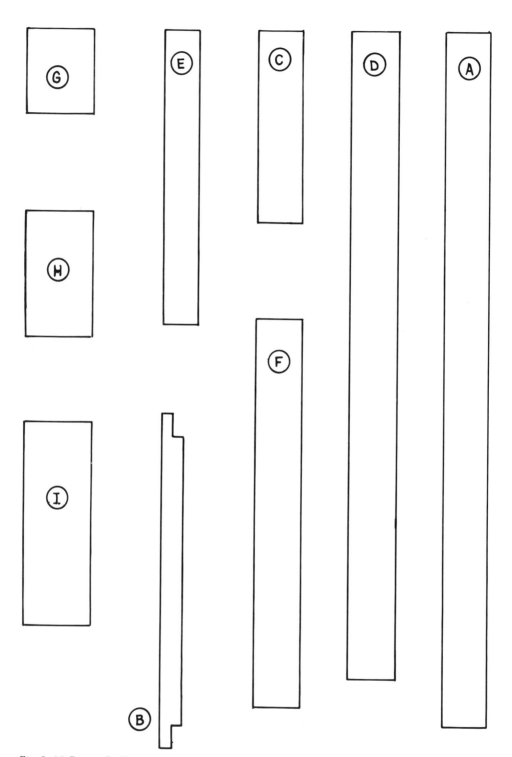

Fig. 9-16 Pattern for Exterior Door

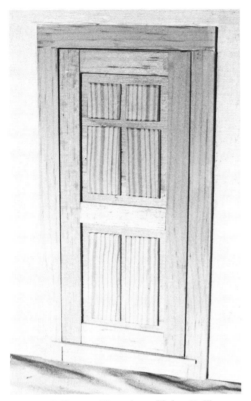

Fig. 9–17 Exterior Door Assembled to Dollhouse

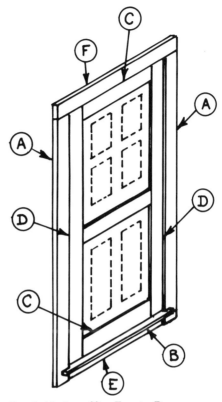

Fig. 9–18 Assembling Exterior Door

of siding flush with the front of the doll-house (Fig. 9–21), and proceed to add additional courses at the previously marked $\frac{1}{2}$ inch increment, overlapping the previous course by $\frac{1}{4}$ inch. Cut to fit at door and windows. (Fig. 9–19) Siding can also be purchased ready made.

SHINGLING THE ROOF

Miniature shingles may be purchased at most hobby stores and retailers of doll-house accessories. If you are inclined to do things for yourself, however, consider making your own shingles.

MAKING SHINGLES

1. Use $\frac{3}{4}$ inch scrap lumber, Knotty cedar or pine. Eight inches wide and 2 or 3 feet long.
2. Set the rip fence on the table saw for $\frac{1}{16}$ inch width, and rip the board length-wise until the board is cut into strips.
3. Adjust the rip fence to $1\frac{3}{8}$ inches (length of shingles) and, with ten or twelve

153

Fig. 9–19 Siding and Door Installed on Dollhouse

strips at a time, cut these strips until you have about 1200 shingles.

APPLYING THE SHINGLES

The first row, or starter course, of shingles needs to be beveled or tapered for a uniform-looking roof. The end can be beveled with a knife. Bevel the end for about $\frac{3}{8}$ inch (Fig. 9–22). This beveling will allow the second row of shingles to lie flat on top of the first row.

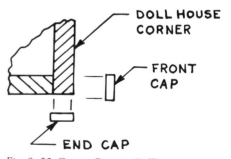

Fig. 9–20 Corner Caps on Dollhouse

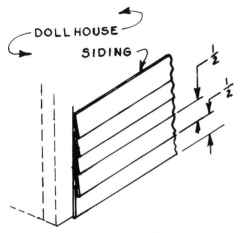

Fig. 9–21 Detail of Applying Siding

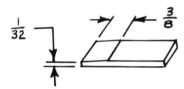

Fig. 9–22 Detail of Beveling Shingle

Measure $1\frac{1}{8}$ inches from the front edge, and draw a pencil line across the entire roof. This will position the top end of the first row (Fig. 9–23). Overlap the first shingle $\frac{3}{16}$ inch from the side of the roof, and proceed to apply the first row of tapered shingles to the roof with glue, spaced $\frac{1}{32}$ inch apart as shown.

Start the second row and all alternating rows with a half-width shingle. Then apply full shingles spaced $\frac{1}{32}$ inch apart $\frac{3}{4}$ inch from the bottom edge of the first row (Fig. 9–23). Continue until entire roof is covered. On the dormers, start at front edge with the first row, and apply shingles as above (Fig. 9–24).

For the final top row, use half-length shingles. Cap this with a strip of wood $\frac{3}{32}$ inch thick by $\frac{3}{8}$ inch wide and as long as required.

The interior walls of the dollhouse can be finished with wallpaper, paint, or paneling, or a combination of wallpapering and paneling.

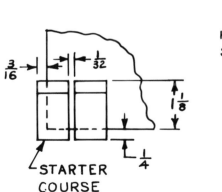

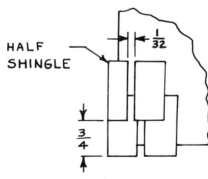

Fig. 9–23 Detail of Starter Course of Shingles

Fig. 9–24 Installing Shingles on Dollhouse Roof

Fig. 9–25 Installing Guard Rail

GUARD RAIL

Once the interior walls and floors have been completed, the guard rail may be installed (Fig. 9–25).

MATERIALS

PART		DIMENSIONS	QUANTITY
A	Post	$\frac{3}{8} \times \frac{3}{8} \times 2\frac{3}{4}$	1
B	Baluster	$\frac{3}{16}$ dia. dowel $\times 2\frac{3}{16}$	9
C	Railing	$\frac{1}{4} \times \frac{3}{16} \times 7$	2

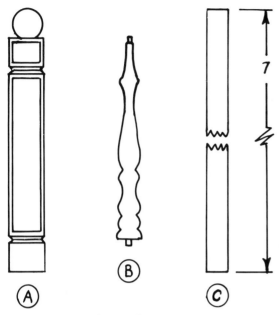

Fig. 9–26 Pattern for Guard Rail

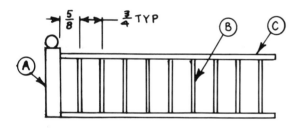

NOT TO SCALE

Fig. 9–27 Assembling Guard Rail

CONSTRUCTION

1. Cut post **A** to length, and shape with a knife (Fig. 9–26).
2. Cut balusters **B** to length, and shape with a knife or wood lathe (Fig. 9–26).
3. Cut railings **C** to length. Then drill $\frac{1}{16}$ inch diameter holes at spacing shown in Fig. 9–27.

4. Sand and stain parts to desired color.

ASSEMBLY

1. Glue balusters **B** between the two railings **C** (Fig. 9–27).
2. Glue baluster and railing assembly to the post **A** (Fig. 9–27).
3. Apply a light coat of spray varnish. Then attach to second floor (Fig. 9–25).

157

CHAPTER 10

Building a Display Case

A display case, or shadow box, is an excellent way to show off the treasures of the miniaturist's furniture collection.

Most display cases are boxes that range anywhere in size from the very small cigar-box size to the larger and more elaborate wall-mounted unit. Small cases have only enough space to house one or two heirlooms. Larger ones

have enough room to contain a lifetime of collecting.

The display case shown in Fig. 10–1 has several features not found in commercially available units. The distinctive roof line is a departure from the stereotype rectangular box. It has a self-contained light source, which allows it to be located anywhere. Finally, it does not

158

Fig. 10–1 Display Case Assembly

use a power transformer, which eliminates the need for an electrical extension cord.

The dimensions for the display case specify $\frac{1}{2}$ inch thick cabinet grade plywood. Following the dimensions listed, this display case will have an inside height of 8 inches, which is equivalent to an 8 foot floor-to-ceiling dimension in full scale. (Note: $\frac{3}{8}$ inch plywood can be substituted for the $\frac{1}{2}$ inch by adjusting the dimensions to compensate for the thinner material.)

CASE FRAME

MATERIALS

PART		DIMENSIONS	QUANTITY
A	*Right End*	$\frac{1}{2} \times 8 \times 13$	1
B	*Left End*	$\frac{1}{2} \times 8 \times 13$	1
C	*Floor*	$\frac{1}{2} \times 8 \times 15\frac{3}{4}$	1
D	*Ceiling*	$\frac{1}{2} \times 7\frac{1}{2} \times 15\frac{3}{4}$	1
E	*Back*	$\frac{1}{2} \times 12\frac{1}{2} \times 15\frac{3}{4}$	1
F	*Roof*	$\frac{1}{2} \times 10 \times 18$	1

In addition to the panels listed above, a 4-foot long piece of picture-framing material 1 inch wide and a piece of standard glass, $8\frac{1}{2}$ inches by 16 inches, are required.

CONSTRUCTION

1. The pattern for the display case is shown in Fig. 10–2.
2. Cut right end **A** to pattern (Fig. 10–3).

159

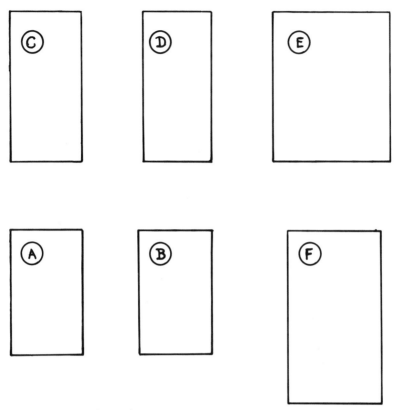

Fig. 10–2 Pattern for Display Case

3. Cut left end **B** to pattern (Fig. 10–3). Reverse the position of the left end before cutting, to match the wood grain with right end **A**.

4. Cut back **E** to dimensions. Then bevel top edge at 30° to match angle of right and left ends.

5. Cut roof **F**, floor **C**, and ceiling **D** to dimensions indicated.

6. Sand edges smooth for a good glue joint.

ASSEMBLY

1. Dry fit parts to assure proper assembly. Then attach, with glue and brads, both ends **A** and **B** flush to ends of the floor **C** (Fig. 10–4).

2. Install ceiling **D** with glue and brads flush with front of ends **A** and **B**, and 8 inches above the floor **C**.

3. Install back **E** flush with ends and floor with glue and brads.

4. Countersink all brads, and fill holes with wood putty. Use sandpaper to remove excess wood putty.

5. Roof **F** will be installed later.

INSTALLING THE PICTURE FRAME

To find the location of the picture frame, face the open side of the display case, measure $\frac{3}{16}$ inch from the inside on both ends, and draw a line the full length of the panels (Fig. 10–5). On the bottom piece, or floor panel, measure $\frac{1}{8}$ inch from the inside, and draw a horizontal line to connect the previously drawn lines on the end panels. These lines will locate the picture framing material. Verify the $16\frac{1}{8}$ inch measurement needed for the glass panel.

To attach the picture frame to the case, select a 4-foot length of 1 inch wide picture framing material, preferably unfinished basswood. Make the first miter cut 12 inches from the left end at 45° (Fig. 10–6).

Align the 12 inch piece of the picture frame with the line on the left hand

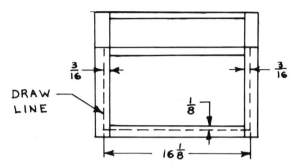

Fig. 10–5 Detail of Picture Frame Layout

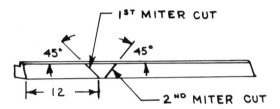

Fig. 10–6 Detail for Cutting the Picture Frame

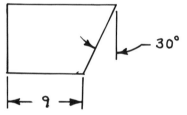

Fig. 10–3 Detail of Display Case End Panels

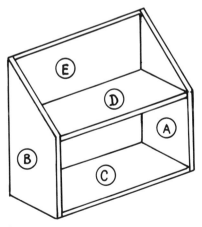

Fig. 10–4 Assembling Display Case

end panel, and temporarily nail in place. (The excess frame projecting above the front of the display case will be removed after the frame has been adjusted to fit.) Reverse the angle, and make a second miter cut at 45° on the same end of the remaining piece of framing. Fit this piece to the miter cut of the first piece. Place frame along the line drawn on the bottom panel. Allowing for the saw blade thickness, find the length across the bottom of the case, draw a line, and cut piece at 45°. Match and cut the remaining piece, and attach along the line drawn on the right end panel. Carefully insert the glass ($8\frac{1}{2}$ by 16 inches) into the frame to check for proper fit. Sufficient clearance has been allowed to permit the glass to slide into place with ease. If the glass binds, adjust the frame position slightly.

161

Attach the frame permanently to the case with glue and finishing nails. Countersink nail heads, and fill the nail holes with wood putty, removing any excess with fine sandpaper. Remove glass, and with a fine-toothed hand saw or table saw remove the excess vertical picture frame at the required angle to match both end panels, allowing the roof panel to fit flush with the case.

(Note: To facilitate handling the glass, cut two pieces of masking tape approximately $1\frac{1}{2}$ inches long and attach to the top edge of the glass, overlapping a full $\frac{1}{4}$ inch on both sides, to form pull tabs. The tabs can be left on permanently, for they will fold back under the roof and hardly will be visible. This will eliminate making fingerprints on the glass while installing or removing the glass from the display case.)

To attach the roof to the display case, fit roof panel flush with edge of the back panel. When centered from either end, there should be a $\frac{5}{8}$ inch overlap. In this position, attach roof to end panel temporarily with 1 inch nails (Fig. 10–7). Refer to Fig. 10–8, and drill a $\frac{3}{16}$ inch diameter hole through the roof panel and $\frac{1}{2}$ inch deep into each side,

located 4 inches from the back edge and $\frac{7}{8}$ inch from each side of the roof.

After both holes have been drilled, remove the roof and enlarge the holes slightly in the end panels only, to accept the $\frac{3}{16}$ inch locating dowels. Then cut two dowels, $\frac{3}{16}$ inch diameter by $\frac{7}{8}$ inch long, apply glue, and insert into the holes in the roof panel so they are flush on the top side of the roof (Fig. 10–9). Slightly taper the projecting ends of the dowels for ease in attaching the roof panel to the display case. *Do not glue roof to the display case.*

APPLYING SHINGLES TO THE ROOF

If you want a shingled roof, refer to Chapter 9 for cutting and installing shingles on the roof panel.

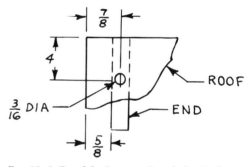

Fig. 10–8 Detail for Locating Dowels for Roof

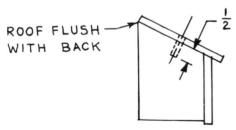

Fig. 10–7 Detail for Locating Roof

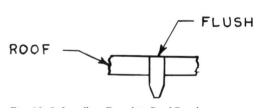

Fig. 10–9 Installing Dowel in Roof Panel

The display case (Fig. 10–10) has a battery-powered chandelier that turns on and off from the exterior-mounted switch in the end panel. There is not sufficient power in this system to flood the display case with light, but it generates a faint, warm glow. The following items are required to install the wiring system:

2 flashlight batteries, size D

1 battery holder

1 switch, toggle or bar

1 chandelier with 3 volt bulb

The battery holder will have to be modified because it is wired for a $1\frac{1}{2}$ volt system (Fig. 10–11). Remove the lead-wire between negative and positive terminals, and solder leadwires as shown in Fig. 10–12.

The following holes will also have to be added to the display case before the wiring system can be installed. Drill a $\frac{1}{8}$ inch diameter hole in the ceiling to accept the electrical wiring for the chandelier $1\frac{1}{2}$ inches from the front of the display case and centered left and right. Next, drill a clearance hole in the end panel above the ceiling height large enough to accept the switch. (Refer to Fig. 10–13 for a wiring diagram of the display case.)

Install the chandelier on the inside of the display case before making the solder connections. When all solder

Fig. 10–10 Assembled Display Case

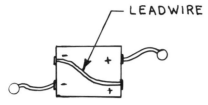

Fig. 10–11 Detail of Battery Holder

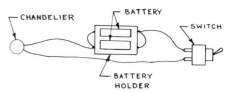

Fig. 10–13 Wiring Diagram for Display Case

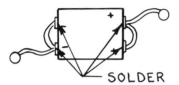

Fig. 10–12 Detail of Modified Battery Holder

connections have been completed, install the two batteries in the battery holder and test the system.

FINISHING THE EXTERIOR

Several options are available for finishing the exterior of the display case.

1. A varnish stain may be applied to match the color of any room decor.
2. Horizontal siding may be applied, as on the dollhouse.
3. Vertical batten strips may be applied to the end panels.
4. End panels may be covered with miniature shingles to match the roof and then stained or painted.
5. A heavy coat of textured paint may be applied to give the exterior a stucco effect.

Another effect may be had by adding a window to one or both ends. (See Chapter 9 for how to build windows.)

FINISHING THE INTERIOR

Wallpaper, in an array of miniature patterns, is available at local specialty shops. Wainscoting may be added with craft sticks. Cut craft sticks to a 3 inch length, stain, and glue to the walls. Then cap the wainscoting with miniature chair-rail molding. Also available are wood-grained papers to simulate wood floors.

If you want something a little different, you may make your own parquet flooring. Take a scrap piece of $\frac{3}{4}$ inch exterior plywood, and with a table saw rip plywood into $\frac{3}{32}$ inch wide strips. Adjust the rip fence on the saw to $\frac{3}{4}$ inch, and rip these strips into $\frac{3}{4}$ inch squares. You now have a scaled 9 inch square wood tile. Simply alternate pattern of the squares, and glue to the floor. Fill any spaces with wood putty and sand smooth. Then apply a coat of clear varnish.

Museums and Publications

MUSEUMS WITH MINIATURE COLLECTIONS

Art Institute of Chicago
Decorative Arts Dept.
Adams at Michigan Ave.
Chicago, IL 60603

Baltimore Museum of Art
Art Museum Drive
Baltimore, MD 21218

The Children's Museum
The Jamaicaway
Boston, MA 02130
17 dollhouses and furnishings. Open by appointment only.

Cleveland Museum of Arts
11150 East Blvd.
Cleveland, OH 44106

Denver Art Museum
100 W. 14th Ave. Pkwy
Denver, CO 80204

Enchanted Doll House Museum
Manchester Center, VT 05255

Henry Ford Museum
20900 Oakwood Blvd.
Dearborn, MI 48121

Frost Museum of Miniatures
Hwy 76, Box 205
Branson, MO 65616
30,000 individual miniatures with authentic backgrounds, including an 1820 Dutch kitchen.

Gift Shop Museum
Cherryville Inn
Cherryville, PA 18035
Santa's workshop in miniature; miniatures from around the world.

Ruth Hackett's Doll Museum
620 W. Jefferson
Kokomo, IN 46901

Hobby City
1238 S. Beach Blvd.
Anaheim, CA 92804

Mott Miniature Museum
Knott's Berry Farm
Buena Park, CA 90620
Includes 66 years of building and represents history of American living; over 150,000 miniature items. Admission charge.

165

Museum of the City of New York
1220 Fifth Ave.
New York, NY 10029

Museum of History & Industry
2161 E. Hamlin St.
Seattle, WA 98112

Museum of Old Dolls & Toys
Winter Haven, FL 33880
Located 1 mile N. of Winter Haven. Features antique dollhouses and dolls spanning three centuries. Shop specializes in furniture and accessories. Admission charge.

Museum of Science and Industry
57th St. and Lake Shore Drive
Chicago, IL 60637
Features Colleen Moore's Fairy Castle: a little palace measuring 9 feet square, with electrical and plumbing systems and more than 1,000 miniatures. Admission free.

Phoenix Art Museum
1625 N. Central Ave.
Phoenix, AZ 85004
Thorne Miniature Rooms, featuring English, French and American period rooms. Admission free.

Smithsonian Institution
Museum of History and Technology
12th and 14th Sts. NW
Washington, DC 20015

The Town of Yorktown Museum
1974 Commerce St.
Yorktown Heights, NY 10598
Features the Marjorie Johnson Dollhouse, a 7' by 8' Victorian. Gift shop. Admission by donation.

Washington Dolls' House & Toy Museum
5236 44th St. NW
Washington, DC 20015
Museum shop features dollhouses, furnishings, books. Admission charge.

Wenham Historical Assn. & Museum, Inc.
132 Main St.
Wenham, MA 01984
Famous doll and dollhouse museum. Admission charge.

NEWSLETTERS AND PUBLICATIONS

Miniature Collector
12 Queen Anne Place
Marion, OH 43302
One year (6 issues) $12. How-to projects, features on craftspeople, suppliers, and hard-to-find books.

Miniature Gazette
P.O. Box 2621
Brookhurst Center
Anaheim, CA 92804
Official publication of the National Association of Miniature Enthusiasts; published quarterly, included with annual $15 membership fee. Special features projects, calendar of events (regional and national), new craft items and interesting people.

Nutshell News
Clifton House
Clifton, VA 22024
One year (6 issues) $12. Editorial articles, new products, new books, fairs, how-to projects, etc.

The Scale Cabinetmaker
P.O. Box 87
Pembroke, VA 24136
A must for the scale model builder. Published quarterly, $12 per year.

Small Talk
P.O. Box 334
Laguna Beach, CA 92651
Published monthly; $12 per year.

Index